A linguistic picture of women's position in society

Bamberger Beiträge zur Englischen Sprachwissenschaft

Herausgegeben von Prof. Dr. Wolfgang Viereck

BAND 17

Verlag Peter Lang
Frankfurt am Main · Bern · New York

Adam Jaworski

A linguistic picture of women's position in society

A Polish-English contrastive study

Verlag Peter Lang
Frankfurt am Main · Bern · New York

CIP-Kurztitelaufnahme der Deutschen Bibliothek

Jaworski, Adam:
A linguistic picture of women's position in society : a Polish-Engl. contrastive study / Adam Jaworski. — Frankfurt am Main ; Bern ; New York : Lang, 1986.
  (Bamberger Beiträge zur englischen Sprach= wissenschaft ; Bd. 17)
  ISBN 3-8204-8979-7
NE: GT

Library of Congress Cataloging-in-Publication Data
Jaworski, Adam, 1957-
  A linguistic picture of women's position in society.
  (Bamberger Beiträge zur englischen Sprachwissenschaft, ISSN 0721-281X ; Bd. 17)
  Bibliography: p.
  1. English language--Sex differences. 2. Polish language--Sex differences. 3. English language--Gender.
4. Polish language--Gender. 5. Sexism in language.
6. English language--Grammar, Comparative--Polish.
7. Polish language--Grammar, Comparative--English.
8. Women--Social conditions. 9. Sociolinguistics.
I. Title. II. Series.
PE1074.75.J39   1986   491.8'5'019   86-10596
ISBN 3-8204-8979-7

ISSN 0721-281X
ISBN 3-8204-8979-7
© Verlag Peter Lang GmbH, Frankfurt am Main 1986
All rights reserved.

All parts of this publication are protected by copyright. Any utilisation outside the strict limits of the copyright law, without the permission of the publishers, is forbidden and liable to prosecution. This applies in particular to reproductions, translations, microfilming, and storage and processing in electronic retrieval systems.

Contents

Introduction	1
Chapter 1 English and Polish gender systems and their relation to sex	5
Chapter 2 Male bias in English and Polish masculine generics	25
Chapter 3 Sex-linked differences in the Polish and English address systems	49
Chapter 4 Sexism in education: Foreign language teaching	67
Chapter 5 Sexism and stereotyping	89
Conclusion	101
Appendix	103
References	107

Introduction

The present work is a contrastive study in linguistic sexism. Both the terms **contrastive** and **sexism** are to be understood here in the broadest sense. The meaning of the concept **sexist language** is partly based on Miller & Swift's (1972) definition of the term. For them, sexist language is "any language that expresses stereotyped attitudes and expectations or assumes the inherent superiority of one sex over the other" (Miller & Swift 1972, quoted in Henley & Thorne 1975:219). Additionally, the term **sexist language** is intended here to cover any form of language use which makes women invisible and unimportant members of society.

The subject matter of this work does not allow for the application of any of the proposed, rigid methodologies for carrying out macro-linguistic (sociolinguistic), contrastive research (cf. Janicki 1979, 1984; House & Kasper 1979; Johnson 1984; Riley 1979). The loosely adopted term **contrastive study** here means the free and fairly unsystematic juxtaposition of certain facts about sexism in English and corresponding Polish phenomena. Thus, my aim has been to show how two different linguistic systems - operating in different societies under divergent social, political and economic conditions - are used to convey and express sexism. Again, the term **linguistic system** is not very precise in this study because it is used here not only in the sense of a rigidly defined system of **grammar** and/or correlation of certain grammatical units with some predefined groups of speakers and situations (Janicki 1984), but also as a socially motivated structuring of one's speech/writing (e.g., the speaker's/writer's decision to describe males' interests as **the** interests of society), and as the inferences one can make about certain uses of language and the presuppositions underlying them.

One of the main reasons why this study is a contrastive one (in the sense outlined above) is that, in English, the study of sexism is a fairly well established discipline with a rich literature[1] and the subject itself is widely taught in Anglo-

American universities.[2] On the other hand, in Polish, this subject has so far received almost no attention and reviewing the work on sexism in English is a necessary preliminary methodological step in researching Polish linguistic sexism.

The work covers a wide range of topics. First, a theoretical foundation for the treatment of grammatical gender as a semantic category is provided and then further evidenced with the experimentally established degree of association of masculine and feminine adjectives in Polish with the gender of (personal) head nouns modified by them (Chapter 1). The implications of this part of the work serve as the basis for a review of the arguments concerning the sexism embedded in the use of the masculine generics in English (man/he) and Polish (e.g. człowiek) (Chapter 2). The issue of sex-linked differences in (American) English and Polish address systems is the theme of the next chapter (3). The following chapter (4) deals with a number of problems concerning sexism and sexist language in foreign language textbooks. The last chapter (5) serves as an overview of some facets of sexism present in different domains of language use: referring expressions, etiquette rules and humour. Some conclusions and suggestions for further research, especially regarding Polish, close the work.

The data used in the present work come from various sources. The English data come solely from the works of other researchers. The Polish data have been collected from different written materials (textbooks, newspapers, etiquette guides, novels, etc.)[3], unstructured observation and informal interviewing of informants, the author's own intuition and introspection, and a few experiments administered to Polish primary-school pupils. Of course, I am fully aware that data which do not result from empirical research may only be used indirectly in describing the sociolinguistic reality of any speech community. However, since the study of sexism in Polish is at such an early stage, the use of methodologies based on intuition are justified by the insights they may provide for future research.[4]

The character of this work is descriptive rather than prescriptive. This means that my aim is to present certain sociolinguistic facts, and not to prescribe the means of changing sexist language. Although I believe that the continuing use of sexist language is socially and politically unjustified - and I express this view later on - much more empirical research and descriptive work in this area is necessary before a decision can be made as to which changes toward nonsexist usage are possible and (psycho-)linguistically desirable,[5] especially in the case of Polish.

This book is based on a revised and slightly shortened version of my doctoral dissertation (Jaworski 1985) and could not have been written without the effort and co-operation of many people. The idea of engaging in research on linguistic sexism came to me during my 1982/83 stay at the University of Florida at Gainesville, where I had the pleasure of auditing two linguistic courses with Dr. M. J. Hardman-de-Bautista. She was the first person who made me aware of the significance of the problem of sexism and to her I owe deep gratitude for her inspiration and the stimulating atmosphere of her classes. I am equally grateful to my research supervisor at the Institute of English at Adam Mickiewicz University in Poznań, Doc. dr hab. Karol Janicki, for his helpful comments on earlier drafts of the dissertation and for his constant encouragement. Prof. dr hab. Jacek Fisiak, director of the Institute, has always provided invaluable encouragement and formal assistance during this and other research projects. I am especially grateful to him for granting me a special research position in 1984/85 which permitted me to devote more time to this work.

Stephen (Szczepan) Krzysztoń shared my enthusiasm for this project when it began in Gainesville and during its closing stages in Poznań. He was also kind and patient enough to correct my idea of written English into the standard, and the task of turning my dissertation into this book became so much easier with his kind permission to use his computer. Prof. dr hab. Lech Hryniewiecki of Karol Marcinkowski Medical School in Poznań provided much appreciated assistance with statistical computations.

I am also grateful to my colleagues and friends who have expressed interest in my work and ideas. Some were hostile, some amused, some skeptical - others, especially Emilia Waśniowska offered helpful support, references and examples. To all of them I owe a better understanding of sexism and the feeling that time has not been wasted.

I would also like to express my thanks to my parents, to whom my debt can never be repaid. My sister and brother-in-law's hospitality at their home in Oxford during September 1984 enabled me to gather a lot of valuable material at Oxford University. They also financed my purchase of a number of books.

The final, but especially dear expression of my thanks and gratitude for assistance, care and understanding in writing this book goes to my wife, Anna.

I am solely responsible for the shortcomings of this work.

Notes

1. See, for example, Hoffman (1980) for a review of some now classic works on the subject of language and sex.

2. Cf. Martyna (1980a) for an outline of suggested topics for teaching 'language & sex' courses.
3. The Polish quotes used throughout this work have been translated by this author. When a quote appears in Polish in the text, its translation follows or is provided in a note.
4. The need for empirical corroboration of often unreliable intuitive data has been expressed and documented by many linguists including Dubois & Crouch (1975), Crosby & Nyquist (1977), and Brouwer, Gerritsen & de Haan (1979).
5. See MacKay (1980) for a discussion of the problems connected with the introduction of nonsexist usage in prescriptive grammars.

1

English and Polish gender systems
and their relation to sex

The English and Polish gender systems differ. The former is said to be 'natural' or 'logical', and the latter is said to be 'grammatical' (Fisiak et al. 1978). In this chapter, however, evidence will be presented that points out that, with regard to English, not all uses or (more importantly) prescribed uses of sex-specific linguistic forms agree logically with the natural gender (sex) of their referents, which indicates extralinguistic conditioning of gender-specific forms in English, and that the Polish gender system possesses some 'natural' characteristics as well.[1] In both systems the status that speakers (and linguists) ascribe to the masculine gender is higher than that given to the feminine gender (cf. Cameron 1985). This fact should prove to have immediate social consequences for English, since the association between grammatical gender and natural gender is more obvious in its gender system than it is in Polish. Nevertheless, as will be shown later, the linguistic category of gender in Polish also has some relevance to extralinguistic reality.

One of the major assumptions underlying the considerations included in this chapter is that the category of gender is not only grammatical but also semantic. This has been suggested by Ervin-Tripp (1976:153) who

> finds that what various kinds of psychological and linguistic evidence suggest is that gender is a property of a semantic content rather than of a word, i.e., is best treated in a theory as part of meaning rather than grammar (Bendix 1979:34, footnote 10).

Such an understanding of gender is also in accord with Miller's (1977) account for the rise of the tripartite masculine/feminine/neuter gender system in Indo-European. He argues that apart from the grammatical reasons for the rise of the feminine gender, there was also an 'external' motivation for Indo-European societies, i.e., the rise and spread of sexism.

This chapter also supports the stance of other authors who maintain that languages that make use of a gender system based on sex need not in themselves be sexist, but may be manipulated so that they embody, reflect and perpetuate sexism (e.g., McConnell-Ginet 1980:5; Bendix 1979). In other words, no language is sexist simply because it has a gender system based on sex. However, if a language or a family of languages, makes sex a **linguistic postulate**[2] (Hardman-de-Bautista 1978), i.e., the speaker's reference to the sex of the person talked about is not only essential, but also unavoidable in an utterance, it has a higher probability of becoming sexist than those which do not have sex as a linguistic postulate. Indo-European languages provide a good example of languages where sex is a linguistic postulate; the Jaqi language of Peru and Bolivia are an example of those which do not have sex as a linguistic postulate (Hardman-de-Bautista 1978).[3]

Linguists differ in their approach to the category of gender depending mainly on their own linguistic framework, as well as on such factors as ideological convictions and their approach to language study, i.e., normative (prescriptive) or descriptive.

For Newmeyer (1983:7), for example, gender is a formal concept which could not be "fully grounded extragrammatically." He attributes no communicative functions to the grammatical gender systems, nor does he ascribe any influence of these systems on conceptual categories. He also argues that one can make no inferences about the differences in the cognition of speakers of different languages who assign opposite genders to the same concepts. Further, he adds that even with human referents gender may show some deviances, as in the often quoted example of the German neuter word das Mädchen ('the girl').

Ibrahim (1973:27) claims that "gender is a linguistic phenomenon and that no extra-linguistic factors were involved in its emergence." For him, gender is, in principle, a morpho-syntactic category, and its essence is in the agreement between the head NP and its determiners, verbal forms, etc. Although he states that the correspondence between natural and grammatical gender is rather poor (e.g., either masculine or feminine nouns may refer to either male or female referents), he also admits that "Gender markers add nothing to the meaning of inanimate nouns, but they are semantically significant in animate nouns" (Ibrahim 1973:97).

Ervin-Tripp (1973a) gives an example of the 'inappropriate classification' of male referents with nouns following feminine declension patterns in Latin and Italian. Syntactically, some of these words are masculine (e.g., il dentista, il poeta), and with these nouns "the force of the deviation is somehow vitiated" (Ervin-Tripp 1973a:158). The deviation may take a more complete form when "a male referent is named by a feminine form which is also syntactically feminine: la guida, la guardia, and la tigre" (Ervin-Tripp 1973a:158). However, these examples of deviant cases do not pose any significant threat to "a tendency to ascribe different connotations to masculine and feminine words in Italian, and [...] the differences are related to the differences in the connotations of gli uomini and le donne (le femine)" (Ervin-Tripp 1973a:167).

Further, Ervin-Tripp states that "In everyday experience, the obvious attributes of objects outweigh any increment of association derived from gender" (1973a:168). This is not always the case, however. In a learning situation, or in an ambiguous situation, the sexual connotations evoked by grammatical gender are fairly significant; in other words, gender carries meaning. Ervin-Tripp (1973a) demonstrates this fact with the results of an experiment in which Italian informants ascribed semantic labels to a number of Italian nonsense-words. The list of the nonsense-words consisted of pairs of masculine and feminine words with exactly the same stem; gender was the only differing factor between the words in each pair. The results were that the masculine and the feminine forms were rated differently, and received different semantic descriptions. The ratings attributed to each word followed the semantic connotations of the words 'men' and 'women' for masculine and feminine words, respectively. Thus, Ervin-Tripp's findings do not fully support Newmeyer's and Ibrahim's treatment of gender as a purely grammatical category.

More support for the idea of treating gender as a semantically-charged category, at least with respect to personal nouns, comes from Fisiak (1963) who says that gender assignment in loanwords (i.e., animate nouns borrowed from English to Polish) also depends on the sex of the referent, e.g., lady, miss, script girl (see also Fisiak 1975).

At this point the following four theoretical principles, which will serve as the basis for further discussion, can be stated:

1. gender is not only a formal grammatical category, but it also carries a (grammatical) meaning which extends into conceptual categories;
2. the distinction of gender based on sex does not result in the Indo-European languages's possession of perfect gender systems since inanimate referents may be referred to with masculine or feminine forms, and male and female referents may be referred to with forms whose gender does not correspond with the referent's sex, but;
3. gender tends to be meaningful in words referring to animate nouns, unknown objects, or in otherwise ambiguous situations, and finally;
4. regardless of whether Indo-European sex-based gender is a result of a linguistic

accident or more or less conscious manipulation of language(s) by its (their) speakers, the category of gender relates to the cognitive structures of extralinguistic reality.

Even in English, which has a 'natural' gender system, there is a need to keep a sharp distinction between grammatical gender and natural gender (biological sex) (e.g., Key 1972; Miller & Swift 1976). Miller & Swift (1976) present the historical development and current usage of some gender specific (e.g., actor/actress) and common gender (e.g., doctor, teacher) nouns in English, and argue convincingly that

> as English made the gradual change from grammatical to natural gender, words denoting occupations or professions could be and from time to time were used for females and males without distinction. But because males are consciously or unconsciously considered the norm, new feminine designations were introduced and accepted whenever the need was felt to assert male prerogatives (Miller & Swift 1976:45).

Consequently, when there are two names for one occupation and one of them becomes a generic term, the other acquires the connotations of referring to a deviation from the norm. The pair actor/actress in English is a case in point. The former is considered a masculine term, the latter a feminine one. However, since actor is also the generic term[4] (as in 'Actors Studio', 'Actors Playhouse'), the real distinction between the two words is not only (if at all, according to Miller & Swift 1976) the one between male and female. First of all, the first term in the pair is socially unmarked and neutral, while the other is marked and expresses a deviation. Secondly, this kind of differentiation "contributes to the overly rigid separation into 'feminine' and 'masculine' of characteristics common to both males and females" and the confusion between the words 'gender' and 'sex' "semantically blur[s] a biological given with something that is socially induced" (Miller & Swift 1976:47). In other words, the feminine gender term (e.g., actress) makes a reference to something which the generic term does not account for.

The apparent confusion between gender and sex is even greater in the English pronominal system. Of special interest is, among other things which will be dealt later, the problem of using the masculine pronoun he (his, him) as the generic pronoun of reference in contexts in which the sex of the referent is ambiguous or unknown (e.g., Each student must sign his own paper.).[5] Stanley (1978) objects to the prescriptive norm of using he as the generic pronoun in English and says that

> There are two ways in which he crept into grammars as the dominant pronoun of reference: (1) because the traditional rule for pronominal

replacement maintains that a pronoun must 'agree with its antecedent noun in gender, number, and person,' and because, according to these [prescriptive] grammarians, most of the nouns in English were masculine, unless marked with a special 'feminine marker'; and (2) when grammarians began to take notice of the 'indefinite pronouns,' anyone, everyone, everybody, etc., they decided that he was going to be the pronoun of reference. Both of these descriptions derive what plausibility they may have from the erroneous equation of gender with biological sex and the correlative assertion that English has a noun classification system based on 'natural' gender (Stanley 1978:802).

This argumentation is partially confusing. It is maintained here that natural gender (sex) should be considered as being distinct from grammatical gender. However, he is an objectionable generic pronoun in English not for the reasons stated above, but because grammatical gender and natural gender greatly overlap in the area of reference to humans with sex-specific forms (such as the pronouns he and she). Otherwise, masculine (grammatical gender) forms would be able to refer to females (sex), and feminine forms to males. If this were true, one could successfully argue that there is nothing peculiar about the use of he in reference to females. Thus, the opinion of the prescriptive grammarians that "most of the nouns in English were masculine, unless marked with a special 'feminine marker'" does not follow from the confusion of gender and sex, but instead from an androcentric world view. Even if most personal nouns in English were masculine, and English had a 'grammatical' gender system, these nouns could refer to females (as, in the most general sense, is the case for Polish).

It is worth noting that in her discussion of the rise and spread of the prescriptivists' opposition to singular pronominal generics other than he, Bodine (1975) does not mention these grammarians' misconceptions about the English gender system, and only gives evidence for socially-motivated prescriptions of sex-indefinite he. Empirical work on the perception (and production) of generic pronouns (e.g., MacKay and Fulkerson 1979; Martyna 1980c) has shown that the masculine generic he tends to be associated and interpreted more as referring to males than to a person of either sex, which is another argument for considering this part of the English gender system as 'natural' and not 'grammatical'.

Perhaps even more important still is the fact that, as Cameron (1985) indicates, the development of the 'naturalness' of English gender has not only been dependent on purely linguistic and sex-reference basis. In her discussion of the attitudes to and beliefs about gender, the actual use of gender specific forms (also in 'generic' contexts), and the relation between gender and sex, Cameron concludes that the relationship between sex and gender is a good deal more complex than the 'all or nothing' of conventional analyses, and is always mediated by ideas of sex difference and male superiority. So-called 'natural' gender in English is not fixed entirely by sex reference but also reflects a variety of ideologically motivated prescriptive practices and folklinguistic beliefs. Conversely, the assignment of 'grammatical' gender in many languages does not depend only on formal criteria. There is a felt connexion with semantic properties of words, and these too are categorised according to ideas about sexual characteristics (Cameron 1985:26).

Further discussion of gender and sex in English, which will later lead to relevant conclusions concerning the Polish gender system, will be based on a summary of research carried out by Mathiot (1979a) and McConnell-Ginet (1979).

Mathiot studied the non-normative patterns of the use of the pronouns he, she and it in English, i.e., how the first two are used to refer to non-human and/or inanimate referents (personification), and how the third pronoun is used to refer to humans (downgrading). Mathiot sees the concept of a **world view** as something to be separated from **referential meaning**. The latter is "the specific information about the world that is directly communicated through linguistic behavior", while the former "is the general way of thinking about the world that underlies all of cultural behavior, including linguistic behavior, and that corresponds to the basic cultural premises of a group. Linguistic behavior, therefore, is one type of cultural behavior that manifests world view. Referential meaning is not world view, it manifests a world view" (Mathiot 1979b:163). Apart from this distinction, Mathiot recognizes two levels of analysis for the study of non-normative (intimate, i.e., used between intimates) uses of he, she and it: **semantic analysis** (corresponding to the study of referential meaning), and **cognitive analysis**, based on the former, but dealing with the concepts underlying the native speakers' use of particular linguistic (here pronominal) items (cf. Manes 1981).

What is important for the purposes of the present argument is the semantic link that Mathiot has unveiled between the use of the pronouns he and she and the inherent role images which native speakers hold about their own and the opposite sex.[6]

As stated above, it is clear that grammatical gender (masculine and feminine) must be distinguished from the biological and semantic concepts of male and female (cf. Bendix 1979). However, viewing sex-based gender as a semantic, and not exclusively grammatical category, one may relate the two. Indeed, Mathiot has found that in the normative pattern the use of the pronouns he and she is not sex-linked, but depends on the biological criterion.

> The non-sex-linked conception of femaleness and maleness is based on a biological criterion, ability to give birth, and presents women as superior to men: women are biologically equipped to do something men cannot do, give birth (Mathiot 1979a:27).

However, the intimate uses of he and she which do not conform to the normative pattern are sex-linked and Mathiot

> is able to uncover semantic elements which lead to a better understanding of how speakers really view masculinity and femininity. For example, objects which represent a challenge are often referred to [...] as she, while women (but not men) apparently consider small, helpless objects to be masculine and refer to them as he ("Will you look at that crazy bird? He's going to break his wings beating them against the window like that!" [41]) (Manes 1981:262-263).

By citing just a few more examples recorded by Mathiot one can see that men, referring to non-human referents with he, present a conception of maleness as **brave** and **good natured** ("a young homeowner described that rabbit with whom he had been fighting for some time as follows: "There he was, just as bold as brass walking through my garden. Nibble here, nibble there. I could have killed him." [38]). When men use she in similar contexts, they express their conception of women as a **challenge** ("A workman trying to fix a key that keeps getting stuck in the lock said: '... that's why she is so hard to turn.'" [38]), and a **prized possession** ("'Let's see how she goes!' (the referent is a new Philco television set [...])" [40]). Women's use of he may express that the referent is perceived as small and cute ("'Isn't he very fragile?' (the referent is a bulletin board)." [41]: cf. also the example quoted by Manes above).

In a related study, McConnell-Ginet (1979) examines the patterns of using singular, third person, generic pronouns in English: he, she, he or she, and singular they. What follows from her discussion is that the prescriptive view which holds that the masculine pronoun (he) is also **the** generic English pronoun, should be re-examined. The prescriptive rule treats he as having the [+masculine] feature, and being neutral with respect to the [+feminine] feature; it is simply 'zero' marked for the feminine feature, since it may embrace female antecedents. In prescriptive terms, she tends to be considered [+feminine] and [-masculine], i.e., it is said to be an impossible generic pronoun. However, McConnell-Ginet shows that she can also be (and actually is) used generically when its antecedent refers to a group of people perceived, in reality, or as a result of a stereotype, to be predominantly female. Compare the following examples in which she is used generically either in reference to a professional group to which mainly females belong (1), or as a clear expression of a social stereotype (2):

1. "When the nurse comes, she'll take your blood pressure."
2. "When a parent hears her baby cry, she rouses quickly."

(McConnell-Ginet 1979:72-73)

McConnell-Ginet also states that the generic he or she has to be used in contexts like: "If either parent in a marriage wants a divorce, he or she (*he) should consult a good lawyer." (McConnell-Ginet 1979:75), since it "is not sex-indefinite but explicitly includes both sexes" (ibid.:74).

Finally, singular they is used generically with antecedents qualified by such quantifiers as every, each and any ("Anyone can pass the exam if they try." [75]), with specific individuals as antecedents ("Someone phoned you this afternoon, but they wouldn't give their name." [75]), and with singular definite generics ("When a person eats too much, they get fat." [76]). Singular they cannot appear, however, with the singular definite generic ("*The child produces many utterances that they could not have heard." [76]). This last example points out that when antecedents are personalized (as is also the case when their proper names are used), they have to be sexualized in our culture, and thus the sexless pronoun they does not fit into the speaker's 'prototypical' concept of the antecedent (cf. Hardman-de-Bautista's [1978] linguistic postulate of sex for Indo-European).

In conclusion, McConnell-Ginet (1979) claims that since he is not the only English generic pronoun, the linguistic analysis should treat she symmetrically with he, and should attribute the feminine pronoun the feature [+feminine] (specific reference), but should also abandon the feature [-masculine] in favour of the feature 'neutral with respect to [+masculine]' (generic reference). What follows from her discussion is that, contrary to the traditional prescriptive rule about the masculine pronoun being the generic one, he is still associated with MALE in whatever context it appears, no matter if the connection between MASCULINE and MALE may be weaker (for adult English speakers) than the connection between FEMININE and FEMALE.

The closing note of McConnell-Ginet's article states the social implications of her own findings:

> Pronouns can refer to real people or to fictive prototypes. So long as most of us believe that women and men are what really exist, that

androgynes are simply abstract entities, we will tend to sexualize our prototype as we personalize them. So long as we obey the edicts of prescriptive grammarians and choose he for sex-indefinite singular antecedents, we prolong the linguistic and sociocultural invisibility of women (McConnell-Ginet 1979:80).

What are the possible implications of these findings for the study of gender in Polish? It seems that at least one hypothesis for Polish can be formulated at present: since Polish is an Indo-European language, which makes sex one of its linguistic postulates, and since, according to prescriptive grammarians, the masculine gender is appropriately the generic one (Klemensiewicz 1982 [1957]), one may suppose that Polish is also a sexist language, i.e., its usage will underrepresent females.

Although the Polish gender system is based on sex and distinguishes nouns as masculine, feminine or neuter, the distribution of the three genders does not always match the sex of the referent. This arbitrariness is especially visible in the case of inanimate nouns which freely take the masculine and the feminine, along with the neuter forms, e.g., ten zeszyt$_m$ ('this notebook'), ta książka$_f$ ('this book'), to pióro$_n$ ('this pen').[7] In other words, gender in Polish is 'grammatical', not 'natural' (Przyłubscy 1983), and according to Grzegorczykowa et al. (1984:154) the sex of the referent is a "secondary feature of this morphological category." This is particularly obvious in the case of inanimate nouns (cf. above). Likewise, the relation between sex and gender is not as rigid in the case of names of animal species (e.g., ptak$_m$ 'bird', pstrąg$_m$ 'trout', ryba$_f$ 'fish', jaskółka$_f$ 'swallow'). Nevertheless, a few animal species have two (or sometimes three) gender forms referring to the respective sexes (and possibly the young), e.g., byk$_m$ - krowa$_f$ - cielę$_n$ ('bull - cow - calf'). The relation between gender and sex becomes even more significant with nouns referring to people (cf. Grzegorczykowa et al. 1984:154).

Despite the fact that gender in Polish is grammatical and, when referring to sexless objects, masculine, feminine or neuter forms can be used, animate referents whose sex is known, or considered relevant, tend to acquire the grammatical gender corresponding to their sex, although, of course, there are deviations from this pattern. What seems important is the fact that native speakers of Polish intuitively consider the masculine gender to stand for what is male and the feminine for what is female. An anecdotal example will illustrate this point. A priest was heard to insist that parents should not teach their children to say Bozinka$_f$ for Bóg$_m$ ('God') for, as he said, "the ending -ka is that of feminine nouns, and God is not a woman" (!).

Similarly, an often quoted example of the interrelationship between gender and cognition is personification (cf. Jakobson 1959, quoted in McConnell-Ginet 1979).

Stories and poems for children abound with personifications which clearly and almost invariably assign sex to inanimate objects depending solely on the grammatical gender of the words which stand for them. Here are just a few examples from a poem ("Na straganie" 'On the vegetable stand') by Brzechwa (1963:87-88) (excerpts):

> Może pan się o mnie oprze,
> Pan tak więdnie, panie koprze.
>
> Mój buraku, mój czerwony,
> Czybyś nie chciał takiej zony?
>
> Naraz słychać głos fasoli:
> "Gdzie się pani tu gramoli?!"
>
> "Nie bądź dla mnie taka wielka"
> Odpowiada jej brukselka.[8]

Note also that Mickey Mouse is a female for most Poles, who associate the sex of this character with the feminine gender of the Polish word $\underline{mysz}_f$ ('mouse').

However, the morphological form of a word or even its syntactic properties do not always determine the perception of its gender. With a large group of nouns which refer to both males and females (the so-called 'common' gender nouns), the grammatical gender assigned to them by linguists is interestingly asymmetrical. Some of these words are morphologically masculine and some feminine, e.g., $\underline{leń}_m$ ('lazy person'), $\underline{śpioch}_m$ ('lie-abed'), $\underline{brudas}_m$ ('slob'), $\underline{sierota}_f$ ('orphan'), $\underline{niemowa}_f$ ('mute'), $\underline{jąkała}_f$ ('stutterer'), $\underline{sknera}_f$ ('miser'). The lexicographers Skorupka, Auderska and Łempicka (1968) provide the following labels for the above listed nouns: the first three are said to be masculine, the next two masculine or feminine with a feminine declension pattern, and the last two are treated as masculine nouns with a feminine declension pattern. This is a clearly sexist interpretation of grammar. All of the above nouns may refer to males and females. The first three agree only with masculine modifiers and verbs (and are truly masculine nouns in this sense), the others, however, may agree either with masculine or feminine modifiers and verbs:

1. ten leń; *ta leń ('this lazy one');
2. ten śpioch; *ta śpioch ('this lie-abed');
3. ten brudas; *ta brudas ('this slob');
4. ten sierota; ta sierota ('this orphan');
5. ten niemowa; ta niemowa ('this mute');
6. ten jąkała; ta jąkała ('this stutterer');
7. ten sknera; ta sknera ('this miser').

If one defines common gender nouns as those which, in the same form, may refer to males and females, i.e., those nouns which, in terms of a 'natural' gender system, are either masculine or feminine, it turns out that Skorupka et al. (1968) treat only nouns (4) and (5) as such. In the case of (1), (2) and (3), although they are used to refer to females, they are not said to be nouns in the common gender. The treatment of nouns (6) and (7) is even more puzzling, since they are not only used to refer to females, but also agree with the feminine forms of modifiers and verbs. In other words, females are excluded completely from the lexicographers' definitions of nouns (1), (2), (3), (6) and (7) and, although the last two nouns are morphologically feminine, the natural gender of males who can be referred to with these nouns overrides the assignment of the feminine gender to them.

The fact that the gender of a Polish word may depend more on whether it can refer to a male person than on its grammatical properties has been observed by Herbert & Nykiel-Herbert (forthcoming). They show that the agreement between a common gender noun and its modifiers depends on grammar when the referent is female (e.g., $\underline{ten}_m$ $\underline{okropny}_m$ $\underline{leń}_m$ Zosia ('this awful lazy Sophia'); $\underline{ta}_f$ $\underline{okropna}_f$ $\underline{sknera}_f$ Anna ('this awful miser Ann'), but tends to be natural when the referent is a man, e.g., $\underline{ten}_m$ $\underline{okropny}_m$ $\underline{leń}_m$ Janek ('this awful lazy John'); $\underline{ten}_m$ $\underline{okropny}_m$ $\underline{sknera}_f$ Marek ('this awful miser Mark'), although $\underline{ta}_f$ $\underline{okropna}_f$ $\underline{sknera}_f$ Marek is also possible.

That the perception of the gender of Polish nouns referring to humans depends on natural gender can be shown with nouns like mężczyzna ('man'), poeta ('poet'), turysta ('tourist'), artysta ('artist'), and some others. These nouns follow a feminine declension pattern but refer specifically to males and, as has been noted, such nouns agree with masculine forms of determiners and verbs (being masculine syntactically) yielding phrases like $\underline{ten}_m$ mężczyzna ('this man'), $\underline{ten}_m$ turysta ('this tourist'), but not *$\underline{ta}_f$ mężczyzna, *$\underline{ta}_f$ turysta, etc.[9] This type of agreement depends purely on the natural gender of the actual/potential referent, and becomes quite obvious when a noun belonging to this group is used to refer to somebody whose sex is not known to the speaker (i.e., the speaker does not realize that the referent is male). Then, agreement will indicate that the noun is perceived as a feminine one, and brings about female imagery. Consider the following advertisement from a Polish newspaper which illustrates the point:

> Sprzedam lampę porcelanową - "siedząca budda".
> (Express Poznański, 29 March 1984)
> ('I'll sell a porcelain lamp - "sitting Buddha".')

The following section presents some empirical evidence supporting the claim that masculine and feminine gender in Polish is, when used in contexts referring to humans, associated with males and females, respectively.

An experiment administered to a group of 47 fifth-graders (24 boys and 23 girls), consisted in the subjects composing and writing down sentences with five adjectives provided for them in the form of an exercise. Three versions of the same exercise were given to the subjects, but each subject received only one version. In Exercise I, the adjectives were given in the masculine form (M), in Exercise II in the feminine form (F), and in Exercise III both masculine and feminine forms (M/F) were provided. Thus, the children made sentences with the adjectives presented to them as in the example below:[10]

Exercise I (M): ambitny;
Exercise II (F): ambitna;
Exercise III (M/F): ambitny/ambitna
('ambitious')

The objective of this experiment was to discover whether in Exercise I (M) the children would produce more sentences referring to or describing males and whether the sentences produced in Exercise II (F) would indicate a parallel female bias. Exercise III (M/F) was used to discover whether the children would balance their use of male and female referents.

The data discussed here include only those sentences which have as their subjects nouns or pronouns clearly referring to males or females in the third person. Common gender nouns, e.g., uczciwy profesor ('honest professor') and generic words, e.g., człowiek ('man' - generic) were excluded from the analyzed data. It is interesting to note, however, that the latter word appeared a few times in some sentences in Exercise I and III, but not in Exercise II. This could be regarded as an indication of a strong male bias for this generic form which, because of its masculine gender, seems not to be associated with the grammatically feminine forms and, consequently, with females (see the following chapter for more details on the use of człowiek).

Table 1. Male and female referents in the sentences of Exercise I and II.

	MALE	FEMALE
Exercise I	36	12
Exercise II	6	37

$\chi^2 = 34.01$, $p < .001$

A Chi-square test of this data shows a very strong correlation between the use of male subjects in the sentences of the exercise in which masculine adjectives were given (I), and a significantly higher use of female subjects when feminine adjectives were supplied (II) ($p < .001$).

Table 2. Male and female referents in the sentences of Exercise I and III.

	MALE	FEMALE
Exercise I	36	12
Exercise III	16	24

$\chi^2 = 11.06$, $p < .001$

A Chi-square test of this data shows a strong correlation between the use of male subjects in the sentences of Exercise I, in which masculine adjectives were given, and a tendency for higher use of female subjects when the adjectives were given in both masculine and feminine forms (Exercise III) ($p < .001$).

Table 3. Male and female referents in the sentences of Exercise II and III.

	MALE	FEMALE
Exercise II	6	37
Exercise III	16	24

$\chi^2 = 7.22$, $p < .01$

A Chi-square test of this data shows a significant difference in the distribution of male and female subjects in the sentences of Exercise II and III ($p < .01$). More female and fewer male subjects were produced in the sentences in Exercise II (F) than in Exercise III (M/F).

Table 4 shows the mean values for male and female referents in the sentences of all three exercises, and presents the "t" values calculated from a comparison of the scores for each possible pairing of the exercises.

Table 4. Mean and "t" values of male and female referents in the sentences of all three exercises.

4a. Exercise I and II (M vs. F)

	I (M) $\bar{X}\pm SD$	II (F) $\bar{X}\pm SD$	t	p
MALE	40.0±19.4	8.6±12.6	5.185	<.001
FEMALE	14.4±17.8	52.8±24.3	4.994	<.001
OTHER	45.6±23.6	38.6±21.4	0.839	>.05

The results in Table 4 show once again that male referents were used significantly more often when masculine rather than feminine adjectives were supplied. The differences in the frequency of occurrence of male subjects in Exercise I and Exercise II, and in Exercise II and Exercise III were not statistically significant. This indicates that male imagery is not elicited as easily by feminine or masculine/feminine adjectives alone. On the other hand, the proportion of female referents rises considerably when the adjectives appear in the feminine or masculine/feminine gender. The data also confirm the hypothesis that the ratio of male and female subjects in the sentences produced by the students would be more clearly balanced in masculine/feminine pairs (Exercise III).

4b. Exercises I and III (M vs. M/F)

	I (M) $\bar{X} \pm SD$	III (M/F) $\bar{X} \pm SD$	t	p
MALE	40.0±19.4	21.3±28.8	2.148	>.05
FEMALE	14.4±17.8	32.0±19.7	2.611	<.05
OTHER	45.6±23.6	46.7±26.6	0.122	>.05

4c. Exercises II and III (F vs. M/F)

	II (F) $\bar{X} \pm SD$	III (M/F) $\bar{X} \pm SD$	t	p
MALE	8.6±12.6	21.3±28.8	1.536	>.05
FEMALE	52.8±24.3	32.0±19.7	2.45	<.05
OTHER	38.6±21.4	46.7±26.6	0.867	>.05

Another experiment, administered to 30 fourth-graders (12 boys and 18 girls) was almost identical to the previous one. A necessary modification, because of the younger age of the subjects, was that the adjectives (here six) with which the children were asked to make sentences, were defined for them. The adjectives were different from those used in the previous experiment. Three versions of the same exercise were distributed among the children participating in the experiment. Each child received only one version and the adjectives were presented to the subjects in one of the following ways:

Exercise I (M): rozważny - najpierw pomyśli zanim coś zrobi;
Exercise II (F): rozważna - najpierw pomyśli zanim coś zrobi;
Exercise III (M/F): rozważny/rozważna - najpierw pomyśli zanim coś zrobi.
('thoughtful - thinks first before doing something')

As in the previous experiment, sentences with subjects other than nouns (or pronouns) in the singular and referring to humans (clearly defined as male or female), were excluded from the analyzed data.

Table 5. Male and female referents in the sentences of Exercises I and II.

	MALE	FEMALE
Exercise I	24	6
Exercise II	7	20

$x^2 = 20.2$, p <.001

A Chi-square test of this data shows a strong correlation (p <.001) between male subjects that appear in the sentences of Exercise I (M) and female subjects that appear in the sentences of Exercise II (F).

Table 6. Male and female referents in the sentences of Exercise I and III.

	MALE	FEMALE
Exercise I	24	6
Exercise III	23	24

$\chi^2 = 9.95$, $p < .005$

A Chi-square test of this data shows a significant difference ($p < .005$) in the distribution of male and female subjects in the sentences of Exercise I and Exercise III. The latter exercise includes more female subjects than the former. Exercise III (M/F) indicates a relative balance in the students' use of male and female subjects.

Table 7. Male and female referents in the sentences of Exercises II and III.

	MALE	FEMALE
Exercise II	7	20
Exercise III	23	24

$\chi^2 = 3.77$, $p > .05$

A Chi-square test of this data shows no significant differences in the use of male and female subjects in the sentences in Exercise II and Exercise III ($p > .05$).

What these experiments have shown is that Polish speakers associate grammatical gender with sex and that masculine gender and feminine gender evoke male and female imagery respectively. This is true at least in an ambiguous or learning situation, as in the case of the exercises described above. This finding seems to be of some consequence regarding the fact that masculine gender forms appear in Polish grammar textbooks more often than feminine ones. Thus, students using these textbooks learn that the masculine gender (associated with male) is the norm, and the feminine (associated with female) is a deviation (cf. Jaworski 1985, Chapter 5).

This chapter has presented some evidence for regarding grammatical gender as a semantically charged category. The acceptance of this view is of considerable consequence for maintaining the claim that if speakers of a language consider the masculine gender 'superior' and 'more comprehensive' than the feminine gender, then they are covertly expressing differing attitudes toward males and females.

Now it is possible to examine the consequences of using masculine gender nouns in Polish as so-called generics and to compare the situation in Polish with the feminist linguistic treatment of the English generics he and man.

Notes

1. This idea is actually not very new. For example, Klemensiewicz (1981), Szober (1962) and Bąk (1978) state that Polish animate nouns possess natural gender.
2. Hardman-de-Bautista (1978:122-123) defines the term in the following way:

    These postulates are those recurrent categorizations in the language which are most directly and most tightly tied to the perceptions of the speakers, those elements which, while language imposed, are so well imposed that speakers consider them just naturally part of the universe, i.e. these are the "rails" upon which thought runs.

3. As is well known, languages without overt sex differences in their pronominal systems may also operate within sexist societies, e.g., Turkish (Gregersen 1979).
4. Clark & Clark (1979:524) treat masculine terms like actor as unmarked and therefore referring to males and females. Feminine terms like actress are considered to be marked and thus to refer only to females.
5. A more detailed summary of research on generic he and man in English is included in Chapter 2.
6. As a matter of fact, women's image of themselves, as revealed in the intimate, non-normative usage of she, has not been studied by Mathiot (1979a:27).
7. To say that there are three genders in Polish requires further explanation. If one treats gender on purely formal morpho-syntactic grounds, the number of genders in Polish can be higher. Corbett (1983) reviews this problem with regard to Polish and, analyzing the data for the types of agreements between nouns and their modifiers and checking relevant case forms of nouns, he comes to the conclusion that six genders should be isolated: masculine personal, masculine devirilized, masculine animate, masculine inanimate, feminine and neuter.
8. Great liberties (hopefully excusable) were taken with the following translation:

    > Maybe you will rest on me,
    > You're withering, Mr. dill.
    >
    > My beetroot, my red one,
    > Wouldn't you like a wife like that?

> Suddenly one hears the bean's voice:
> "Where are you struggling to, ma'am?!"
>
> "Don't act like a big shot"
> Brussels sprout answers her.

9. Although I say here that phrases like *ta mężczyzna are deviant, one can sometimes hear them in playful or otherwise marked usage. It would be interesting to investigate the conditions under which such phrases are used. One of the possible findings of such a study might be that feminine gender agreement with the masculine nouns of the type mężczyzna, turysta, etc. is used to insult or downgrade the male referent (e.g., ta straszna aktorzyna Janek, 'this awful actor John').
10. The complete versions of these and other exercises used in the experiments described in this and the following chapter are provided in the Appendix.

2

Male bias in English and Polish masculine generics

The focus of the present chapter is on the male bias evoked by the use of so-called generics in English: man (men) and he (his, him), and in Polish, with special emphasis on the word człowiek ('man' - generic). The arguments for treating the masculine generics in English as sexist, i.e., discriminating against women by excluding them from the potential/actual reference of these words, will be presented in an overview of work carried out by other researchers. The male bias of the Polish generic człowiek and a few other masculine generics in Polish will be demonstrated by analyzing contexts in which these words may and do appear, contrasting the usage of these words with other, non-generic ones, and presenting the results of a modest empirical study testing the degree to which Polish speakers associate the masculine generic człowiek with other masculine generic forms.

The problem of male bias connected with the use of generic man and he in English has received a considerable amount of attention (cf., for example, Lakoff 1975; Bate 1975; Miller & Swift 1976; Nilsen 1979; Bodine 1975; Martyna 1980b; Silveira 1980; Burr et al. 1972; McConnell-Ginet 1979; Sullivan 1983; see also Kramer et al. 1978; Spender 1980; Smith 1985; and other references in Henley & Thorne 1975).

The use of masculine generics (especially he) has been prescribed by normative linguists since 1795 (Bodine 1975; Stanley 1978) which, of course, does not mean that this usage has always been fully accepted. Earlier, the singular generic pronoun they (their, them) was also widely accepted (Bodine 1975), and man used to be a true generic as it was once possible to use it in reference to females. Miller & Swift (1980:9) observe that "Ercongata, the daughter of a seventh-century king, is described in The Anglo-Saxon Chronicle as 'a wonderful man'." The consequent widespread use of the generic masculine (GM) words in English is seen by most feminist linguists as a reflection and/or result of androcentrism in society and prescriptive linguistics (Miller 1983; Bodine 1975; Silveira 1980).

GM words inadequately serve as true generics and this is apparent on different levels: linguistic, psychological, social and behavioural. These levels are all closely connected with each other and an overview of the problems associated with them will now be presented.

Miller (1983) objects to the grammar rule that states that "Since <u>anyone</u>, <u>everyone</u>, <u>someone</u>, <u>everybody</u>, <u>somebody</u>, <u>anybody</u> and <u>nobody</u> are singular, the singular pronoun <u>his</u> is used with them: **Anyone can apply for <u>his</u> (not <u>their</u>) license.**" (BSIG 1976:51), and claims that "the **form** of this alleged rule assumes that there is only ONE 'singular pronoun' par excellence, and that is the MALE pronoun <u>he</u>" [emphasis his] (Miller 1983:178). Indeed, the above prescriptive rule is in disagreement with the reality of English which has always made use of singular <u>they</u> as a possible generic pronoun. Bodine (1975) provides some examples of English sentences in which <u>they</u> performs this function:

(1) Anyone can do it if they try hard enough. (mixed-sex, distributive)
(2) Who dropped their ticket? (sex unknown)
(3) Either Mary or John should bring a schedule with them (mixed-sex, disjunctive) (Bodine 1975:131).

She also cites four more sentences containing the generic <u>they</u>, which contradict the rule quoted by Miller. From these examples one can easily deduce that impersonal pronouns need not always be 'singular' and, even when they are, <u>they</u> can be co-referential with them:

(4) Did everyone say they missed you like mad yesterday?
(5) Somebody left their sweater.
(6) Not one single child raised their hand.
(7) When you call on a student, it's better if you can remember their name.

In (4), then antecedent of 'they' has a plural meaning, but the antecedents of 'they' in (5), (6), and (7) are clearly singular. Notice particularly (6) and (7). If subjects were perceived as plural, surely the speakers would have said 'their hands' and 'their names' rather than 'their hand' and 'their name' (Bodine 1975:139).

Similarly, Nilsen (1979) argues that <u>they</u> can function as a generic pronoun no matter if its antecedent (an indefinite pronoun) is understood as plural or singular:

> For example, if I come home from school and find my dining table covered with books and papers, I shout out 'Someone left their books on the table!' I definitely have in mind a plural reference - my son, my husband, my daughter, and perhaps various friends. In this particular situation, I would not consider saying, 'Someone left his or her books on the table.' If I had found only one pile of books on the table, I might have used this statement, but probably not. For the sake of efficiency and tact I would most likely have relied on the identical [...] 'Someone left their books on the table!' although I would have had a singular referent in mind (Nilsen 1979:368).

Miller & Swift (1980) state that children can be quite logical and they quote an anonymous teacher who said: "I corrected a boy for writing 'no one ... they' instead of 'no one ... he', explainig that 'no one' was singular. But he said, 'How do you know it was a he?'" (1980:36). On the other hand, children must perceive adults as illogical and inconsistent when it comes to the use of GM words. An example is provided by Clarricoates (1978):

> During my observations a teacher of 7 year olds asked the children to write down an example of a mammal and to give a particular feature that marked it off from other types, such as amphibians. Imagine the look on her face and the increased confusion of the child as she tried to explain why his wasn't exactly right when Peter had written:
> 'Man is a mammal. He breastfeeds his young.'" (1978:360).

Miller & Swift (1976) have more to say about the confusion children may experience acquiring the generic vs. specific connotations of the GM forms man/men. They quote the full definition of these words from The Golden Picture Dictionary for Beginning Readers (1972) as follows: "Man, men - A boy grows up to be a man. Father and Uncle George are both men." After this they say:

> A child may infer from this that mother and Aunt Jane are not men. Nobody, least of all a very young child, learns the meaning of man from a dictionary, but this limited definition does fit the child's experience. A word means what it means not because of what dictionaries say about it, but because most speakers of the language use it with a certain meaning. If Billy, at age three or four, were to see the 'Avon lady' coming up the front walk and say to his mother 'Here comes a man,' she would correct him. If at nursery school he were asked to draw a picture of a man and he drew a figure that appeared to be a woman, he might be carted off to a psychiatrist.
> In primary school, however, children begin to encounter man and men in contexts that include people like mother and Aunt Jane and the Avon lady. And despite a conflict with the meaning they already know, they are expected at this stage to acquire an understanding of the other, so-called generic meaning of man (Miller & Swift 1976:21).

Young children are not the only ones who are confused about the suitability of GM words in certain contexts. "Startled laughter often greets such sentences as 'Menstrual pain accounts for an enormous loss of manpower hours ...'" (Martyna 1980b:489). Two other widely quoted examples indicate that the pseudogeneric word man is predominantly associated with males:

> Man can do several things which the animal cannot do. ... Eventually, his vital interests are not only life, food, access to females, etc., but also values, symbols, institutions ...
>
> As for man, he is no different from the rest. His back aches, he ruptures easily, his women have difficulties in childbirth ... (quoted in Miller & Swift 1980:12).

Miller (1983) quotes a few more examples of this kind and provides his readers with adequate comments:

> 'Victorian Man was a creature of sexual ignorance; he visited prostitutes, believed that women had no sexual feelings, and put vinegar-soaked sponges in his vagina to prevent conception.' (!!!)
>
> The bizarreness of this last example lies in the use of he in specifically feminine contexts. Another example of this type is cited by Penelope (Stanley) 1979:35 from the 'No Comment' section of Ms. (Dec., 1978:102):
>
> 'If anybody believes that "the Safe Period does not work for everybody," he can be assured that the Ovulation Method will give him the certainty he seeks and which he was unable to find in the Rhythm Method ...'
>
> If he were a generic pronoun, there would be nothing strange about using it in female contexts. [...] **That he strikes us as bizarre in specifically female contexts is proof that it is not generic** [emphasis his] (Miller 1983:173-174).

Significant support for treating GM words as false generics comes from empirical research (see, for example, Martyna 1980c; Schneider and Hacker 1973; MacKay & Konishi 1980; MacKay & Fulkerson 1979; Silveira 1980). Huddleston (1984:290) states that when he is used in a sentence like "If any student wishes to take part in the seminar, he should consult his tutor.", the semantic distinction between female and male is neutralized. However, this claim does not find support in psychological reality. Moreover, the perception and production patterns for the use of generic he and other generic pronouns (they, he or she) are different for males and females.

Martyna (1980c) has found that female college students use he (in its generic function) fewer times than male college students do. This difference became apparent in different linguistic contexts: when the antecedent was associated as stereotypically male (police officer), stereotypically female (secretary), or neutral with respect to sex (human being). To determine whether the use of the generic pronoun he resulted from male imagery associated with particular antecedents, the students were asked whether this was indeed the case. While 60 percent of the men who used he in the neutral context said 'yes', only 10 percent of the women did so. This indicates that men associate generic he with their own sex more readily than women, and it is easier for them to picture hypothetical 'generic' persons as male, whereas women's use of he in such contexts indicates that they do it both for the lack of better choices and to stay within the norms of grammatical standards and patterns of correctness. (MacKay & Fulkerson 1979 found similar sex differences in the production of generic pronouns.)

In another experiment reported by Martyna (1980c), college students were presented with complete sentences containing one of the generic pronouns (he, they, he or she), and each sentence was followed by a picture showing a male or a female. Martyna's hypothesis was that if he were a true generic pronoun, the pictures of males and females should be equally applicable as illustrations of the sentences containing the generic he. "Yet, nearly 20 percent of the students said a formal picture did not apply to a sentence containing the generic he" (Martyna 1980c:73). Increasing the students' awareness of the presence of the generic he in the test sentences by presenting them to the students simultaneously with the pictures, Martyna found that "approximately 40 percent of the students reported that the female picture did not apply to the sentences with generic he - about twice the number in the previous study" (1980c:74). Martyna further notices that:

> Altering a few contextual factors so that the he was more readily noticed doubled the ambiguity and sex-exclusiveness of generic he. Had the experiment been designed to approximate the occurrences of he in everyday contexts, that percentage would undoubtedly have been higher" (1980c:74).

MacKay and Fulkerson obtained similar results in their studies, and have concluded that "generic he readily conveys the male interpretation but not the female interpretation" (1979:666). When Schneider and Hacker (1973) asked some 300 students to bring pictures illustrating different chapters of a hypothetical sociology book, the students produced a significantly larger number of male pictures than of males **and** females when the chapter headings contained the GM word man (e.g., "Urban Man", "Industrial Man", "Economic Man", etc.) rather than when the titles did not contain the word man (e.g., "Urban Life", "Industrial Life", "Economic Behavior", etc.).

Studying the use of pronouns in children's literature, MacKay and Konishi (1980) discovered, among other things, that the pronouns he and she are used to personify non-human referents in a way that indicates covert and overt stereotyping of females and males. In addition, the pattern of personification of non-human objects in children's literature indicates that "the peripheral status and infrequent mention of she animals" (MacKay & Konishi 1980:160) in the works studied reflects the non-existent status assigned to women by the prescriptive GM he. Other empirical research following different methods of collecting data has confirmed the results mentioned above (see Silveira 1980 for a review of these experiments).

In spite of the evidence suggesting very strongly that English GM words render women invisible, strong opposition still exists to the abandonment of sexist usage and the adoption of alternative ways of referring to human beings in generic contexts. (See Blaubergs 1980 for a review of the arguments against changing sexist language.) Researchers are also aware of serious psycholinguistic problems which may prevent the alternative pronouns (e.g., they) from replacing the GM he in prescriptive grammar (MacKay 1980). Stylistic reasons (e.g., he or she being considered clumsy), may also be responsible for the avoidance of alternative usages and hinder change. Some linguists (e.g., Lakoff 1975) claim that avoiding sexist pronoun usage in English is not conceivable because pronouns are "too common, too thoroughly mixed throughout the language, for the speaker to be aware each time he uses them. It is realistic to hope to change only those linguistic uses of which speakers themselves can be made aware, as they use them" (Lakoff 1975:45). However, as Bodine (1975) observes, a number of European languages (including English) have changed their pronominal systems, and the various "analyses of change in second person pronoun usage rank among the most convincing demonstrations of the social motivation of linguistic change" (Bodine 1975:142). And as Abbott (1984) demonstrates with the example of her analysis of actual uses of they in generic contexts in contemporary English, new rules that would include they as a possible generic pronoun should also be incorporated in prescriptive grammars for foreign students of English.

An important new direction toward the avoidance of sexist usage in English is indicated by the fact that various publishing houses and professional groups have issued special guidelines for non-sexist language for their writers/members (see, for example, American Psychological Association 1977),[1] and as Cooper (1984) and his associates have shown, in some types of written American texts there was a significant move toward the abandonment of GM words.

It is possible now to turn to an analysis of the use of Polish GM words, most notably the word człowiek ('man' - non-generic). Its relation to the feminine gender generic word osoba ('person') and the non-generics mężczyzna ('man' - non-generic) and kobieta ('woman') will also be considered. The data come from dictionaries, unstructured elicitation of judgements from native speakers of Polish, actual usage found in written materials, the author's intuition, and an empirical study examining the relation between the grammatical gender of Polish generics and the gender of other personal nouns co-occurring with them.

The two most commonly used personal nouns in Polish which serve the generic function are the masculine człowiek and the feminine osoba. Dictionary definitions of the two words vary considerably in their length and scope. For example, Skorupka et al. (1968:519) give the following definition of the word osoba: "a human individual, man - generic, a character." This definition is followed by a list of a few phrasal expressions in which the word osoba occurs and two other meanings of the word are provided: "grammatical person" and "a character in a play." The word człowiek has seven definitions and a long list of phrasal expressions in which it can occur. The meanings of człowiek in Skorupka et al. (1968:98) are as follows:

> 1. Homo sapiens, the most developed species in the order of primates, having - unlike other animals - the ability to think, speak, make tools and use them in collective work [...] 2. a person representing the best human traits, a socially valuable individual, ethical, noble [...] 3. in the function of the personal pronoun ja ['I'] or in the function of the indefinite pronouns ktoś ['someone'], ktokolwiek ['anybody'], every undefined subject [...] 4. a grown-up person [...] 5. coll. dated worker, labourer [...] 6. dated servant, subject [...] 7. coll. man (non-generic).

In the framework adopted here, both generics could be regarded as having an equally discriminatory value: osoba being a feminine noun creating female imagery and being a false generic discriminating against men, and człowiek being a masculine noun having a male bias, consequently discriminating against women. However, the meaning of both generics is not identical, the range of contexts in which they occur differs, and the word człowiek appears to be used as an intended generic word more often than osoba.

If, then, one accepts it that człowiek and osoba evoke male and female imagery respectively, and człowiek is used in a wider set of contexts, discrimination against women takes place more often than against men.

Indeed, in most of its uses osoba resembles an indefinite pronoun (this meaning is not separately listed for osoba in Skorupka et al., but cf. def. 3 for człowiek quoted above). With this semantic restriction on the use of osoba, it is hard to use this word when speaking of human beings in general, referring to people as a biological species (homo sapiens - def. 1 of człowiek above), and human beings as individuals having ethical, social and other virtues (def. 2 of człowiek above). Consider the following examples:

Myślisz, więc jesteś człowiekiem.

*Myślisz, więc jesteś osobą.

('You think, therefore you are a human being/person.')

Zachowuj się jak człowiek.

*Zachowuj się jak osoba.

('Behave like a human being/person.')

Further, osoba cannot be used in specific reference to an (unknown) person unless it is additionally qualified, for example, by the demonstrative pronoun ta_f ('this'), just like the indefinite pronoun ktoś ('someone') has to be preceded in such contexts by ten_m ('this'). No such restriction holds for człowiek. Compare:

Zostaw człowieka w spokoju.

Zostaw tego człowieka w spokoju.

*Zostaw osobę w spokoju.

Zostaw tę osobę w spokoju.

*Zostaw kogoś w spokoju.

Zostaw tego kogoś w spokoju.

('Leave [this] human being/person/someone alone.')

That linguists treat the word osoba more like an indefinite pronoun rather than a personal noun is also implicitly revealed by Tokarski's (1978) exclusion of this form from his analysis of nouns in the semantic field CZŁOWIEK.

According to definition 3 above, człowiek can function to mark the speaker (in place of the pronoun ja ['I']); this reading of osoba is also largely constrained, since the first person pronoun has to have a specific referent and osoba does not function in this way (unless additionally qualified in some restricted contexts). Compare:

Człowiek nie może tego słuchać.

*Osoba nie może tego słuchać.

('One [= I] cannot listen to this.')

but

Moja osoba nie może tego słuchać.
('My person cannot listen to this.')
Osoba does not mean 'an adult, mature person', the way człowiek does (def. 4 above). Compare:
"Dzieckiem straciłem go z oczu; człowiekiem ujrzałem na powrót" (Doroszewski 1958-1969, Vol. I: 1148).
*Dzieckiem straciłem go z oczu: osobą ujrzałem na powrót.
('I lost sight of him when he was a child, but saw him again as a man/person.')
Finally, the dictionary states (def. 7 above) that człowiek also means mężczyzna, but it does not say, however, that one of the meanings of osoba is kobieta.

Herbert & Nykiel-Herbert (forthcoming) state, though rather inconclusively, that "osoba has only a true generic reading and does not suggest female referent" while "the grammatically Masculine noun has developed a dual function (1. generic, 2. male)" (Herbert & Nykiel-Herbert forthcoming). Rothstein (1976:252) states that the noun człowiek serves as an example of a masculine noun with an unmarked masculine gender function because it is possible to say "Pani Marta jest wzpanialym człowiekiem" (' [Ms.] Martha is a wonderful human being.'), but in specific reference, when człowiek appears in a syntactically independent position its interpretation is specifically male: "Czeka na ciebie jakiś człowiek." ('Some man is waiting for you.'), "Nie znam człowieka." ('I don't know the man.'). In his parenthetical remark to his definition of osoba Doroszewski (1958-1969, Vol. V:1142) adds that, in the singular, it is more often used to denote a woman. Interestingly enough, in his definition of człowiek there is no (even parenthetical) remark that this word has also the non-generic reading.

In sum, the female imagery suggested by osoba appears to be less frequent than the male imagery evoked by człowiek.

The following section will examine some of the example sentences used by Doroszewski (1958-1969) to illustrate the various meanings of the word człowiek. None of the uses of this word is regarded by Doroszewski as specific (i.e., non-generic). In the 24 "człowiek" sentences used by Doroszewski, 15 refer to humans of unspecified sex, 16 to males and only two are used in sentences referring to females. Fifteen sentences in which the word człowiek explicitly or implicitly refers to males were selected for further analysis. In these sentences, the word człowiek is used as a specific reference to individuals and/or in certain fixed expressions:

1. To najuczciwszy człowiek pod słońcem, nikogo nie bił, uratował życie wielu więźniom.
('This is the most honest man under the sun; he has not beaten anyone and has saved many prisoners' lives.')
2. Romantyczny obraz tego artysty (Chopina) jaki przekazała nam legenda, sposób w jaki przez długi czas pojmowano jego utwory, zasłoniły nam człowieka z krwi i kości, często rozbawionego jak dziecko.
('The romantic picture of this artist (Chopin) handed down to us in legend and the way in which his works have been understood have prevented us from seeing the man of flesh and blood [who was] often amused like a child.')
3. Walił "dwóje", ale był człowiekiem gołębiego serca i wszystkich ze swojego otoczenia za podobnych siebie uważał.
('He gave failing grades, but he had a heart of gold and considered everyone around him to be like himself.')
4. Staruszek nie rozumie pewnych rzeczy, jest człowiekiem starej daty.
('The old man does not understand certain things; he is an old-fashioned man.')
5. Tadeusz Kościuszko to przede wszystkim człowiek czynu.
('Tadeusz Kościuszko was first of all a man of action.')
6. W Dłutwie był kościół niedaleko dworu i stary ksiądz proboszcz, poczciwości człowiek, typ dawnych jeszcze proboszczów, pełen prostoty i nienarzucającej się, nie wojującej wiary.
('At Dłutwa there was a church near the manor-house and an old parish-priest, a most kind-hearted man, a typical old parishoner, full of simplicity and self-effacing, of a non-militant faith.')
7. W Karolu zbudzila sie duma młodzieńca w którym mimo zupełnej dojrzałości duchowej, świat nie chciał widziec człowieka.
('The pride of youth awakened in Karol, who, despite his complete spiritual maturity, was not regarded by the world as a man.')
8. Dzieckiem straciłem go z oczu, człowiekiem ujrzałem na powrót.
('I lost sight of him when he was a child, but saw him again as a man.')
9. Ojciec pani, zacności człowiek, dziwnie przypadł mi do serca.
('Your father, most worthy man, had a strange fascination for me.')
10. Atencji okazał się godnym, umiał bowiem roztoczyć uroki człowieka światowego, popisać się wykształceniem, koligacjami świetnymi i zamożnością.
('He turned out to be a man of note, as he was able to present himself as a man of the world, to show off his education, his excellent connections and wealth.')

11. Wierz mi, człowiek ten próżny, zepsuty i hardy, nie zemsty, ale raczej godny jest pogardy.
('Believe me, this vain, spoiled and proud man is not worthy of revenge but only of contempt.')
12. Syn to bardzo zacnego człowieka, rzekł Pan Podolski.
('He is the son of a very fine man, said Mr. Podolski.')
13. Wypadało do wielkiej tej sprawy wprowadzić człowieka z głową.
('It was only right to choose for this major task a man with a good head on his shoulders.')
14. Człowieku, ależ to pół pensji pójdzie na to manko. Z czego będziem-y żyli? Człowieku, coś ty narobił? Ja po prostu ochłonąć nie mogę z przerażenia.
('Hey, man, this short-fall will cost someone half of their salary. What are we going to live on? What have you done, man? I simply can't cope with the awfulness of the situation.')
15. Dlaczegóż, mój człowieku, nie prosisz od razu i na papierosy?
('Man, why don't you come to the point and ask for the money to buy cigarettes?')

Since, as has been stated, all of the 15 sentences refer to males, or can be so used, the question arises as to whether they can be used in reference to females. In order to test this, the sentences were slightly rewritten by changing or adding personal names, names of professions, feminine verb endings, etc., so that the word człowiek in each sentence would explicitly refer to a female:

1a. To najuczciwszy człowiek pod słońcem, nikogo nie biła, uratowała życie wielu więźniom.
2a. Romantyczny obraz tej artystki jaki przekazała nam legenda, sposób w jaki pojmowano jej utwory, zasłoniły nam człowieka z krwi i kości, często rozbawionego jak dziecko.
3a. Waliła "dwóje", ale była człowiekiem gołębiego serca i wszystkich ze swojego otoczenia za podobnych siebie uważała.
4a. Staruszka nie rozumie pewnych rzeczy, jest człowiekiem starej daty.
5a. Hanka Sawicka to przede wszystkim człowiek czynu.
6a. W Dłutwie był klasztor niedaleko dworu i stara matka przełożona, poczciwości człowiek, typ dawnych jeszcze przełozonych, pełna prostoty i nienarzucającej się, nie wojującej wiary.
7a. W Marii zbudziła się duma dziewczyny, w której mimo zupelnej dojrzałości duchowej, świat nie chciał widzieć człowieka.
8a. Dzieckiem straciłem ją z oczu, człowiekiem ujrzałem na powrót.

9a. Matka pani, poczciwości człowiek, dziwnie przypadła mi do serca.
10a. Atencji okazała się godna umiała bowiem roztoczyć uroki człowieka światowego, popisać się wykształceniem, koligacjami świetnymi i zamożnością.
11a. Wierz mi, człowiek ten próżny, zepsuty i hardy, nie zemsty, ale raczej godny jest pogardy. Cóż innego można o niej powiedzieć?
12a. Syn to bardzo zacnego człowieka, rzekł Pan Podolski i dodał o niej kilka ciepłych słów.
13a. Wybrano Marię, ponieważ wypadało do wielkiej tej sprawy wprowadzić człowieka z głową.
14a. W końcu Jan powiedział do niej: "Człowieku, ależ to pół pensji pójdzie na to manko. Z czego będziemy żyli? Człowieku, coś ty narobił? Ja po prostu ochłonąć nie mogę z przerażenia."
15a. Zapytał Marię: "Dlaczgóż, mój człowieku, nie prosisz od razu i na papierosy?"

Four Polish informants were then consulted on the acceptability of the rewritten sentences, and they were asked if the word człowiek was better, equally good, or worse sounding in these sentences than the word kobieta. The informants' judgements yielded the following results: (1) Sentences 11a, 12a and 15a were found unacceptable when the word człowiek was used to refer to a female and the word kobieta was chosen to replace it. (2) In sentences 1a, 7a, 8a, 9a, 10a, 14a, although they were generally accepted when referring to females, the informants strongly preferred the word kobieta to the word człowiek. (3) Człowiek and kobieta were found to be equally suitable when referring to females in sentences 3a, 5a and 6a. (4) The word człowiek was strongly preferred to kobieta in sentences 2a, 4a and 13a. These results indicate that in some contexts the supposedly generic word człowiek is not the most suitable term of reference for females.

In further analysis, the informants were asked to evaluate the use of mężczyzna as a replacement for the word człowiek in the original 15 sentences. The replacement of człowiek by mężczyzna in the sentences in question did not produce parallel judgements to those obtained for the sentences in which kobieta was preferred when referring to females. The word mężczyzna was found acceptable in only two sentences (7 and 8), whereas in the remaining thirteen sentences mężczyzna was found to be either totally unacceptable or at least less favoured than the word człowiek.

Comparing the results of the judgements of the two sets of sentences (with the word człowiek used to refer to females and the word mężczyzna instead of człowiek used to refer to males) one may conclude that (1) If all 15 sentences contained the word człowiek in one of its generic senses, it should be possible to use it with an equal degree of acceptability in reference to men and women (for example, the way człowiek functions in 2, 2a, 4, 4a, 13, and 13a). However, for most of the sentences, when they refer to women, native speakers' intuitions suggest the use of kobieta rather than człowiek. The explanation of this fact here is that człowiek has a strong male bias, and therefore, when speaking of women, seems too ambiguous, if not totally contradictory to the intended message. (2) In parallel sentences człowiek is preferred over mężczyzna when referring to males, and kobieta is preferred over człowiek when referring to females. Thus, even when the word człowiek is used intentionally as a generic, in some contexts it acquires an exclusively male interpretation which makes the use of the word mężczyzna redundant, since it is needlessly sex-specific. (3) As (1) and (2) suggest, człowiek is a pseudo-generic in many of its uses, since in specific reference it is most readily interpreted as referring to males only.

The use of masculine generics in Polish may be ambiguous **and** confusing with respect to the actual sex of the person being discussed. Nalibov illustrates this problem:

> "Jak już pisałem, Seidler jest reporterem kontrowersyjnym, o wielkich ambicjach i nie cofającym się przed trudnościami i niebezpieczeństwami." (Kupiszewski 1967:374)
> Barbara Seidler is the author of the book Dziś na wokandzie (Today on the Court Calendar) from which Prof. Kupiszewski cited the preceding passage. Taken out of the context of the book in which it appears, it is impossible to determine from this passage whether Seidler is a man or a woman (Nalibov 1973:19).

Not only is it impossible to determine the sex of the person spoken about in the passage, but any attempt at disambiguating the sex of the referent will produce a male interpretation. Out of context, the only "natural" reading of masculine generics (here: reporter) is in favour of males.

One of the most blatant ways of excluding women from one's speech or writing in Polish is to restrict the meaning of the supposedly generic word człowiek to mean 'male'. Człowiek = 'male' and ludzie = 'males' in the following example in which Rem (1984) explains why a collection of his essays bears the title Felietony dla cudzych żon ('Essays for the wives of others'):

> Felietony te recenzowane są często, ale ustnie. Ludzie podobnej co autor orientacji politycznej spotykając go wygłaszają zadziwiająco jednorodną formułę: "Wiecie, Urban, wasze felietony są mocno kontrowersyjne, ale moja żona je czyta i bardzo chwali".

> Dlaczego żony służą do czytania tych tekstów? Być może sprawia to ostrożność. Człowiek doświadczony sam woli, się zbytnio nie angażowac, więc wypycha przodem kobietę (Rem 1984:5).³

In this passage <u>ludzie</u> = 'males' because only males can say that <u>their</u> wives read somebody's essays, and <u>człowiek</u> = 'male' because the sentence would not make any sense if <u>człowiek</u> also meant 'female' here and would mean something like: "An experienced man or woman does not want to get involved so he or she lets the woman have a first go."

Rem also tells his readers that only males die in Poland:

> Lektura nekrologów wskazuje [...] że co drugi nieboszczyk w Polsce umiera jako osoba wybitna, choć za życia te jego walory nie zaaznaczały się w takim stopniu jak w nekrologach i uchodził za byle kogo. W każdym razie owe nekrologi sugerują, iż prawie każde mieszkanie po nieboszczyku da się przemienić w muzeum, a wdowie można zapewnić etat kustosza opiekującego się kałamarzem, trzema fotografiami oraz krzesłem, na którym zmarły siadywał (Rem 1984:34).⁴

The male imagery of masculine generics seems to be unquestioned. The linguistic invisibility of females within these terms is partly a result of the masculine gender imposing its semantics on the speaker's/writer's cognition (though this point needs, of course, further psychological corroboration with the use of empirical methods), and the traditional way of treating male as the norm and female as a deviation. Despite the often seen and heard clichés that females have attained full equality (educational, professional, legal, etc.) the average Pole remains <u>Jan Kowalski</u> ('John Doe'). At least in everyday, popular speech and writing, a male represents the Polish nation.

Some more examples of male bias present in the thinking of authors writing in Polish will provide useful illustrations of the problem.

The article from which the following quote is provided is addressed to an average Catholic man or woman. It comes from a religious journal whose readers consist of males and females, but the latter may have a considerable problem identifying with the narrator of the text:

> Jestem już zmęczony zarówno tyloma pytaniami jak i samą pracą. Jestem głodny, znudzony i zły. Właśnie w takim wściekłym nastroju wracam do domu. I tu przepraszam, ale jeszcze kilka pytań: przede wszystkim - czy przygotowuję 'powrót do domu'? Czy wracam zatruty zmęczeniem, kompletenie bezmyślnie? Jedynym moim marzeniem jest zjeść i wyciągnąć się w fotelu z gazetą w ręku. Mógłbym co prawda w modlitwie połączyć się ze św. Rodziną z Nazaretu i zapytać się: co to

znaczy, że ja mam żonę, dzieci? Czy ja traktuję ich, tych żywych najbliższych mi ludzi, gorzej niż kolegów z pracy? Czy ja kogoś nie uprzedmiatawiam? Czy moich bliskich nie traktuję zbyt instrumentalnie? Mają mi podać jedzenie (to żona - współpartner sakramentu) i dać ... święty spokój (to dzieci - wynik świętego sakramentu - związku małżeństwa)? (Pawłowski 1983:83).

The following two examples illustrate similar, sexist imagery embodied in the plural form of człowiek - ludzie ('people'). To my knowledge, no Polish dictionary says that one of the possible meanings of ludzie is 'male human beings':

> Porad w intymnej dziedzinie udzielają doświadczeni seksuolodzy i psycholodzy. Najwięcej zgłoszeń przypada na miesiące letnie, gdyż o tej porze roku problemy seksualne wzrastają - ludzie przebywają na powietrzu, kobiety zaś ... prowokują skąpymi strojami[6] (Gazeta Poznańska, 9 September 1983, No. 213, p. 8).

In this quote ludzie acquires a male bias when it is contrasted with the phrase kobiety zaś ('while women'). In the following text the principle on which ludzie acquires a male bias remains the same, although the contrasting word here is dziewczyny ('girls').

> Młodzi ludzie, starsi panowie, panie, dziewczyny, uczniowie, studenci, emeryci, wszyscy którzy chcą wzmocnić swój budżet, poświęcają godzinę, dwie, trzy, temu zajęciu (Express Poznański, 13 October 1983, No. 201, p. 1).

The sexist bias of Polish will now be illustrated in the context of the exclusion of women from the anthropological record of the early stages of the evolution of human kind. Tanner (1981) has shown that the role of women in evolution (especially their significance in food-gathering, tool-making and the development of communication) has been largely neglected. (For example, see Stopa 1983 for his justification of tracing the etymology of the word for 'father' but not for 'mother' in the Hottentot-Bushman languages.) An example of such underrepresentation of women is found in a handbook of biology (Skowron 1973) in which the author first says that, in contrast to the other hominids, only males hunted in early human societies (with no mention made of what the females were doing at that time) and then states that hunting was the only possible cause for the development of erect bipedalism, since hunting required running and the simultaneous use of tools. Considering this information, one would conclude that the erect position of the human body is uniquely a male contribution, which the females imitated or developed in some other mysterious fashion. What this hypothesis does not consider, however, is that women, who were the most active gatherers and actually provided up to 70% of the food consumed by their communities (this fact is completely ignored in the handbook in question), like the men, had to cover long distances, and their hands must have been occupied as well (cf. Tanner 1981; Dahlberg 1981).

Apart from the word człowiek, one may point out other, so-called generic words (personal nouns), which, despite their masculine gender, are said to refer equally to both men and women (Klemensiewicz 1982a [1957]), though they turn out to be sexist. The following examples indicate that the use of such masculine generics leads to (1) the creation of exclusively male imagery, and (2) an uncertainty as to whether the word refers to both males and females, or only to males, and thus adding to the linguistic invisibility of women in Polish.

The first example illustrates the sexist use of the word czytelnik ('reader'). This word is used in the salutation drogi czytelniku ('dear reader') referring to male and female readers. However, what follows indicates that males are the sole addressees of the salutation:

DROGI CZYTELNIKU
    Kiedy speceruję po parku widzę na ławkach przytulone do siebie pary młodych, myślę: może ten blondyn ostrzyżony na jeża - to jesteś Ty, a ta dziewczyna w niebieskiej wiatrówce, którą tak czule trzymasz za rękę - to Ona (Kozakiewicz 1962:5).[8]

A sentence from an introduction to another book (Townshend 1976) shows a similar sexist bias:

    Każdy kierownik, a więc także i polski, może w tej książce - jak w zwierciadle - zobaczyć jakiś rys swój własny, swojego szefa, kawałek swojego biura, przedsiębiorstwa, nawet swoją żonę ... (Martyniak 1976:8).[9]

And another quote indicates that when someone leaves their family it must be a man:

    Znane są [...] nie tylko psychiatrom, ale i w praktyce normalnego życia przypadki, kiedy na skutek szaleńczego zakochania porzuca się spokojną rodzinę, dzieci, kochającą żonę, dobrą posadę ... (Witczak 1984:58).[10]

If Polish masculine generics were completely ambiguous as to the sex of their referents, there would be no special need for writers (or speakers) to make additional comments when their intent, when they use one of the so-called generics, is to include women. On the other hand, if men were the intended referents of the generic words, it would also be necessary to add specific information. However, it is only when one wants to speak about women that additional specific information about the meaning of the generic word is required (and actually used):

W sąsiednim gmachu na parterze urzęduje sekretarz rady, kobieta (Bohdziewicz 1981:178).
('In the neighbouring building on the ground floor is the office of the secretary of the council; a woman.')

Celnicy (a widzę przede wszystkim celniczki) tkwią jeszcze na swoich miejscach, coś piszą (Radgowski 1983:5).
('The customs officers [and I predominantly see female customs officers] are still in their places, writing something.')

If this use of celnicy ('customs officers') were not sexist the following paraphrase of the above sentence would be possible:

*Celnicy (a widzę przede wszystkim celników) tkwią jeszcze na swoich miejscach, coś piszą.
('The customs officers [and I predominantly see male customs officers] are still in their places, writing something.')

One of the main contentions of this chapter has been that masculine generics in Polish embody a strong male bias which leads to the use of sexist language. In the light of the findings of the previous chapter, it is possible to hypothesize that the masculine gender of Polish generics is the principal linguistic factor responsible for the male imagery associated with these words. If this claim is valid (i.e., if it is true that masculine gender = male bias), then the following report on an empirical study testing the degree of association of the Polish generics człowiek and osoba with other nouns with which they are co-referential will be another, though indirect, proof that masculine and feminine gender terms are responsible for creating either male or female imagery.

The aim of this experiment was to find out if there is any possible correlation between the grammatical gender of the Polish generics człowiek and osoba and the gender of the nouns used co-referentially with them, that is, if the subjects were more likely to use masculine nouns in sentences with the word człowiek, and more feminine nouns with the word osoba.

The subjects were 116 fifth and sixth-graders (57 boys and 59 girls) attending an elementary school in Poznań. Each child completed one of the three different types of 'lexical' exercise. The subjects' task was to guess and write down the names of professions defined for them in 15 sentences/definitions. With the exception of the beginning phrases used to introduce the sentences, the definitions in all three exercises were identical. For example:

Exercise I
1. Człowiek, który leczy chorych to ....
2. Człowiek, który uczy w szkole to ....
('The man who cures the sick is called ....')
('The man who teaches at school is called ....')

Exercise II
1. Osoba, która leczy chorych to ....
2. Osoba, która uczy w szkole to ....
('The person who cures the sick is called ....')
('The person who teaches at school is called ....')

Exercise III
1. leczy chorych - ....
2. uczy w szkole - ....
('cures the sick - ....')
('teaches at school - ....')

Exercise III was administered in order to test if there would be any significant differences in the use of masculine and feminine nouns when no clue to the gender of a 'prototypical' professional was provided.

The comparison of mean values for the masculine (M) forms and the feminine (F) forms in the three exercises above is presented in Tables 1,2 and 3. Table 1 compares Exercises I and II; Table 2 compares Exercises I and III; and Table 3 compares Exercises II and III.

Not all of the answers given by the subjects tested yielded clear-cut M or F results. Some children provided both forms in some slots (marked M/F in the Tables), left some slots blank, or wrote their answers illegibly (these fall under the category "other" in the Tables). The percentages of "M/F" and "other" categories do not show any significant differences in the exercises.

Table 1. Comparison of M and F forms in Exercises I and II

	Exercise I $\bar{X}\pm SD$	Exercise II $\bar{X}\pm SD$	t	p
M forms	73.2±10.76	60.5±11.26	4.961	<.001
F forms	22.6±10.34	37.1±11.17	4.199	<.001
M/F	0.7± 2.06	1.1± 3.33	0.594	>.05
Other	3.4± 7.31	1.1± 2.94	1.773	>.05

A t-test of this data shows a strong relationship between the use of either M or F forms depending on the generic word introducing the definition of a profession. More M forms were used by the subjects to complete the sentences starting with człowiek (Exercise I) rather than with osoba (Exercise II) (p <.001), and significantly fewer F forms were used to complete sentences in Exercise I than in Exercise II (p <.001).

Table 2. Comparison of M and F forms in Exercises I and III

	Exercise I $\bar{X}\pm SD$	Exercise III $\bar{X}\pm SD$	t	p
M forms	73.2±10.76	65.1±14.81	3.07	<.01
F forms	22.6±10.34	33.3±10.42	4.099	<.001
M/F	0.7± 2.06	0.9± 4.31	0.181	>.05
Other	3.4± 7.31	0.7± 2.52	2.177	>.05

A t-test of this data shows a stronger tendency to use M forms with sentences introduced by the generic word człowiek (Exercise I) than with those sentences which have no introductory generic word (Exercise III) (p <.01). The percentage of F forms in Exercise I is also significantly smaller than in Exercise III (p < .001).

Table 3. Comparison of M and F forms in Exercises II and III

	Exercise II $\bar{X}\pm SD$	Exercise III $\bar{X}\pm SD$	t	p
M forms	60.5±11.26	65.1±14.81	1.176	>.05
F forms	37.1±11.17	33.3±10.42	1.925	>.05
M/F	1.1± 3.33	0.9± 4.31	0.268	>.05
Other	1.1± 2.94	0.7± 2.52	0.602	>.05

A t-test of this data shows no significant differences for the use of either M or F forms between Exercises III and II. This indicates that the association of M and F forms with the generic word osoba is practically the same as when no generic word is used to introduce the sentences.

Summing up the above results, it is possible to say that the generic word człowiek increases the perception of male imagery on the part of the subjects (reflected in a more frequent use of M forms in Exercise I), and that the generic word osoba increases female imagery (Exercise II), though not to a point which would be significantly different from the 'distribution' of male and female imagery associated with the names of professions when no generic word is used (Exercise III).

Table 4 presents the data and the "t" values calculated from the mean percentages of M and F forms used in each exercise based on the subjects' sex. These results show that the only statistically significant differences for boys and girls in the three exercises (p < .05) results from the higher percentage of F forms used by girls in Exercise I (człowiek) and in Exercise II (osoba). In the remaining cases the differences were not statistically significant.

Table 4. Mean values for boys and girls in the three exercises

Exercise I	boys $\overline{X} \pm SD$	girls $\overline{X} \pm SD$	t	p
M forms	75.9± 7.75	70.1±13.09	1.724	>.05
F forms	19.7± 7.75	26.2± 7.74	2.427	<.05
M/F	0.3± 1.46	1.1± 2.57	1.84	>.05
Other	4.1± 9.3	2.6± 4.06	0.626	>.05
Exercise II				
M forms	63.2±11.39	58.2± 9.1	1.319	>.05
F forms	33.3±10.17	41.1±11.5	2.129	<.05
M/F	1.4± 3.56	0.7± 3.13	0.616	>.05
Other	2.1± 3.87	---	---	---
Exercise III				
M forms	69.4±10.56	62.8± 9.81	1.864	>.05
F forms	29.4±10.83	34.1± 9.78	1.518	>.05
M/F	0.4± 1.63	2.2± 4.34	1.674	>.05
Other	0.8± 2.23	0.9± 3.05	0.067	>.05

However, a Chi-square test of the results obtained from summing up all instances of M and F forms used by boys and girls in all three exercises (Table 5) shows that there is no overall tendency for girls to use more F forms and fewer M forms than for boys (p <.005). Although it is not possible to draw any definite conclusions from this modest finding, I would suggest that females, more than males, see feminine gender nouns as suitable for performing the generic function. Consequently, this might be a sign that females try to linguistically mark their presence in the social world.

Table 5. M and F forms used by boys and girls in Exercises I, II and III.

	M forms	F forms
Boys	596	232
Girls	557	297

$x^2 = 8.91$, $p < .005$

The linguistic near-invisibility of women in "generic" contexts can occur and be tolerated only in a society whose world-view discriminates against women. Are the Polish masculine generics responsible for a sexist world-view or do they merely reflect it? One may as well argue over the primacy of the chicken or the egg. There is no doubt, however, that the linguistic sexism of Polish does reinforce the social inequality of the sexes.

This chapter has presented evidence that GM words are false generics in both English and Polish. It appears that, in both languages, GM words evoke male imagery and tend to be associated much more with other masculine gender nouns. This male-centred usage of GM words calls for socially motivated language change. While successful attempts in this direction have been made in English, Polish needs much more descriptive work regarding sexist usage in order to bring about similar results.

Notes

1. For a comprehensive discussion of arguments for change in favour of non-sexist language see Martyna (1980b). For the psychologist's opposition to sexism in general see Albee (1981).
2. As I have written, Seidler is a controversial reporter with great ambitions who will not retreat in the face of difficulty and danger.

3. These essays are often reviewed but [only] orally. People with a political orientation similar to that of the author's, when they meet him, express a surprisingly uniform opinion: "You know, Urban, your essays are very controversial, but my wife reads them and praises them very much." That is why this is titled Essays for the wives of others.
   Why do wives read these essays? Maybe because of caution. An experienced man does not want to get overly involved, so he lets the woman have a first go.
4. A reading of obituaries indicates that every one of the deceased in Poland was an outstanding person, though during his lifetime his virtues did not stand out to the degree that they do in the obituaries and that he was considered a nobody. In any case, these obituaries suggest that almost every apartment left by a deceased person can be transformed into a museum, and that his widow can be guaranteed the position of custodian in order to care for the ink-pot, three photographs and the chair on which the deceased used to sit.
5. I am already tired of so many questions and of the work itself. I am hungry, bored and angry. In just such an angry mood I am returning home. But here, sorry, there are a few more questions: first of all - do I prepare the "homecoming"? Do I return poisoned with exhaustion, completely unthoughtfully? My only dream is to eat and stretch out in an armchair with a newspaper in my hand. As a matter of fact, I could in a prayer join the Holy Family of Nazareth and ask: what does it mean that I have a wife, children? Do I treat [them], these living people who are the closest to me, worse than my colleagues at work? [...] Do I not treat them too instrumentally? They are to serve food to me (my wife [...]) and leave me in peace (my children).
6. The advice on this intimate matter is given by experienced sexologists and psychologists. Most inquiries are made in the summer months since in this time of the year sexual problems grow - people stay out in the open air, while women ... provoke [them] with little clothing.
7. Young people, elderly men, women, girls, pupils, students, retired pensioners, all those who want to back up their budgets devote one, two, or three hours to this occupation.
8. DEAR READER
   When I am walking in the park I can see young couples cuddling each other on the benches and I think: perhaps this blond-haired man - this is you, and the girl in the blue jacket whose hand you are holding so tenderly - this is she.
9. Each manager, even a Polish one, may see in this book a mirror image of his own characteristics, those of his boss, his office, his business, or even his wife.
10. There are cases not only known in psychiatry but also in the practice of everyday life, when after madly falling in love one abandons a peaceful family [life], children, a loving wife, a good job.

3

Sex-linked differences in the Polish and English address systems

Forms of address have traditionally been recognized as linguistic indicators of the social relations holding between the addresser and addressee, and reflecting their relative statuses (cf., among others Brown & Gilman 1972; Lyons 1977; Trudgill 1974; Hudson 1980). Writing about English vocative NPs, Zwicky argues that they "are almost never neutral: they express attitude, politeness, formality, status, intimacy, or a role relationship, and most of them mark the speaker" (Zwicky 1974:796). The principle of non-neutrality of forms of address seems also to apply to Polish nominal and pronominal forms of address[1] used in direct or indirect address.[2] Based on these assumptions, any analysis of the use of forms of address in any language (though here the focus is on English and Polish) should reveal that if any two groups of people within one speech community[3] have different repertoires of forms of address and receive different (or socially non-equivalent) forms their social identity and status are different, and often unequal.

A number of problems in the American English address system have been revealed which indicate that in this area of language behaviour, women and men act differently. This fact has not always been recognized by researchers working on the American address system (cf. McConnell-Ginet 1978 with reference to Brown & Ford 1961). Traditional models have reflected male to male usage to the exclusion of female to female or cross-sex patterns.

McConnell-Ginet distinguishes the differences between men and women as addressers and addressees from three viewpoints: "1) inventories [repertoires], 2) semantic systems, and 3) developmental cycles" (McConnell-Ginet 1978:26). Some of these differences are summarized below:

1. <u>Inventories</u>. Men, as addressers, appear to have larger repertoires of forms of

address than women do. In non-familiar relationships more men than women use socalled 'generic first names' (FN): Mac, Buster, Joe, and Mary, Grace, Ella, of which the last three are used among male homosexuals. Other 'bonding terms' include: buddy, pal, amigo, friend, brother and man, and some which are overtly insulting but are also used in situations of camaraderie: dude, turkey, son-of-a-bitch, motherfucker. These forms, when used by women, imply an insult.

The far fewer, seemingly parallel forms used for women are more restricted in usage. Toots and lady (similar to the generic FNs) are more readily used to address familiars. Bitch is used in a similar way with women as dude is used with men (insults and situations of friendship). Kid, kiddo and babe are more often used by men with women than by women with women, and the last of the three 'bonding terms' mentioned here is used by men only when the addressee is a non-familiar woman.

Likewise, women, as addressers, have smaller repertoires for addressing others in casual and non-intimate though friendly situations. The singular and plural terms: sir, ma'am, miss, ladies, girls, and guys which women use, are also used by men. Men more often address non-familiar women with forms derived from physical characteristics: e.g., blondie and chestie.

The use of a last name (LN) alone is more typical of male to male than female or cross-sex address. Women as addressers have a wider range of FNs, most of which are sex-specific. Some of them are sex-ambiguous (graphically and/or phonologically), and when they first become so, they have a tendency to no longer be used with males (e.g., Evelyn, Joyce). Some feminine names are derived from masculine FNs by the use of special feminine suffixes (Jamesetta, Georgenia). Opposite processes do not occur. Further differences deal with the use of kin titles. Son and brother are used as forms of address by non-kin more often than by kin. Daughter is not used as a form of address, except within a family, when it is part of a larger phrase (e.g., my darling daughter). Father has virtually been abandoned as a form of address, whereas Mother (less frequent than Mom) has not. Occupational titles "are sex-preferential because most occupations are sex-typed: Judge and Doctor stand beside Teacher and Nurse" (McConnell-Ginet 1978:28). Social titles are not only distinguished by form, but also by number. There are three titles for women (Mrs., Miss, and Ms.) and one for men (Mr.).

Two major conclusions follow from the above survey of American English nominal forms of address: 1. men have larger repertoires of forms of address and can be addressed with a greater variety of forms than women, and 2. most uses of forms of address identify the addressee as male or female (McConnell-Ginet 1978).

2. Semantic systems. Where the inventories of male and female forms of address differ, the semantic values of given forms also tend to differ. However, even where they overlap, the meaning of particular forms depends on the sex of the addresser and addressee. An obvious example of semantic differences in the 'parallel' male/female forms of address is provided by the social titles mentioned earlier. Mr. is applicable to all adult (or perceived as adult) males, while the choice of the appropriate female title depends on the addressee's marital status (Miss vs. Mrs.) and/or the addresser's (and addressee's) ideology (Miss and Mrs. vs. Ms.).

McConnell-Ginet (1978) quotes a number of examples indicating that a female is more likely to receive an FN in situations where a male of equal status would receive a more deferential term (like title+last name [T+LN]), and she also mentions the possibility that sometimes an FN used by an inferior woman to a superior woman may indicate their greater solidarity and not necessarily the former's lack of respect for the latter.

In the case of endearments such as dear, honey, darling, baby, love, "men receive them only from intimate women whereas women receive them from everybody" (1978:32). In their empirical study, Wolfson & Manes (1980) elaborate on the use of endearments for women. They analyzed forms of address received by women in service encounters and discovered that, unlike men who in equivalent situations received the respectful sir from service clerks, women were frequently addressed with terms of endearment. The types of situations in which terms of endearment are used with women by service clerks, and the fact that these forms are also used by adult intimates and non-reciprocally by adults with children, indicate that "along with any connotation of friendship involved in the use of terms of endearment in service encounters, goes the additional implication that the addressee is subordinate to the speaker in some way, just as a child is subordinate to an adult" (Wolfson & Manes 1980:90).

Bodine (1977) stresses the role of sex in the uneven distribution of forms of address in American English and warns against overemphasizing other social dimensions (e.g., status and age) in accounting for sex-linked differences in address patterns,

> since non-reciprocal naming between women and men occurs even when there is no status differential or when the woman is of higher status, in the occupational sense. In the past year, this reviewer [i.e., Bodine] has heard 'Ann, this is Mr X' (Mr X identifying himself on the telephone) from a lawyer ten years my junior, an insurance agent of my same age, an older carpenter, and a university supply clerk of unknown age. Each 'Mr' was fully aware that 'Ann' is also a university professor. Language, because of

its concreteness, recordability, and relative ease of analysis, appears to be a particularly good behavioral domain in which to explore whether sex exists as a social dimension in and of itself or only as a contributor to the differential distribution of females and males among other, (nonsex) roles (Bodine 1977:105-106).

3. Developmental cycles. Unlike girls, boys entering school initiate an exchange of LNs in certain contexts which performs a number of social functions (e.g., bonding). Later, with varying degrees of intensity, this mode of address is retained by men throughout their lifetimes. For women, the exchange of LNs, if ever occurs at all, is strongest "in late adolescence or early adulthood", and when "LN does occur to females, it appears to be associated with typically masculine or masculinizing contexts" (McConnell-Ginet 1978:33).

Among the most powerful insults used for boys are female names that are phonetically similar to the addressee's real name (Paulette for Paul, Donna for Don, etc.). Girls are called with masculine names more seldom and even then, this is not insulting.[4]

LNs and multiple names mark off boys' transition from 'babyhood' to 'manhood' and are important in their socialization process. The forms of address girls start receiving in early adolescence are: "generic endearments and sex-marked address from non-familiar males" (McConnell-Ginet 1978:34). A new title (Mrs. vs. Miss) and a new (husband's) LN signal the beginning of a woman's adulthood; an experience not paralleled by boys and young men. A woman who adopts Ms. for self-identification may have problems retaining this title after the adoption of her husband's LN and even more so after having children that bear their father's LN.

Kramer (1975) has also pointed out sex-linked differences in the American address system. She has examined a number of literary sources and cartoon captions, and has used data from actual occurrences of address forms in one type of service interaction and from self-reported data of males and females from different age groups. Her data confirm McConnell-Ginet's and Wolfson & Manes' findings. In the literary works consulted for the purpose of her study, Kramer found that men address women and men more often and with a greater variety of terms than women address other women and men. The same holds true for customer-clerk relations.

> Female students were addressed in service encounters by female salespersons as 'dear' and 'miss' and by male salespersons as 'seniorita', 'ma'am', 'lady', 'kiddo', 'young lady', 'sweetie', 'little lady', 'miss', 'dear', 'lovely' and 'baby'. Male students were addressed by female salespersons as 'sir' and 'dear' and by males as 'sir' (Kramer 1975:203).

Mister was another term of address reported in Kramer's study to have been used for males by other males in stores and in restaurants.

Kramer points out that within a dyad, the person who uses more forms of address to the other is often dominant in the situation. She also argues, on the basis of her literary data, that "since addressing often appears in the literature to be a sign of aggression we can hypothesize that in actual speech women are addressed more than they address" (Kramer 1975:206).

The conclusion Kramer reaches is that the asymmetry in the way that males and females address each other, both in available repertoires and frequency, reflects the existence and maintenance of the asymmetry of the social rights of men and women.

Polish forms of address have not been studied and described as thoroughly as English, but even in the few studies available it is possible to observe a male bias in the way that the rules for the use of Polish address forms are stated. This bias is in most cases very subtle, but provides enough evidence to show that in this area of sociolinguistic behaviour, male is treated as the norm and female as a deviation from it, sometimes not even worth mentioning.

Pisarkowa (1979:8) states that there are seven "substitutes for 2nd person pronouns" (i.e., nominal forms of address used in place of 2nd person pronouns and usually co-occurring with the verbal forms in the 3rd person singular),[5] and she lists the following forms: pan ('sir'), obywatel ('citizen'), kolega ('colleague'), towarzysz ('comrade'), druh ('companion/boy scout'), ksiądz ('priest'), and ojciec ('father'). This list is not comprehensive for two reasons. First of all it does not include the feminine counterparts of these forms, which, with the exception of ksiądz, all exist: pani ('ma'am'), obywatelka, koleżanka, towarzyszka, druhna, and matka ('mother'). This may mean that Pisarkowa treats the masculine forms as generic, i.e., including both male and female referents (addressees). This is surprising in the light of the fact that no native speaker of Polish would maintain that pan also includes pani or that ojciec includes matka. Later in her discussion, Pisarkowa mentions feminine forms used in indirect address, indicating that her original list of seven "substitutes for pronouns" was meant to include the feminine forms. Another, equally mistaken reason why Pisarkowa did not bother to include the feminine "substitutes" in her list might have been that the masculine and feminine forms follow the same usage for male and female addressees, respectively. (That this is not the case will be discussed later.) One way or another, Pisarkowa regards the feminine forms as being of secondary importance to the masculine ones. And finally, if Pisarkowa had meant to subsume the feminine forms under the masculine ones, she should have noticed that the form ksiądz has no feminine counterparts. In sum, it appears that when Pisarkowa gave her list of the "substitutes for pronouns", she thought in line with the male norm and underrepresented female usage.[6]

The second reason why the list of seven "substitutes" is not comprehensive is that there are more than just the seven Pisarkowa listed (if one accepts the very concept of "substitutes for pronouns"). She herself mentions forms like brat ('brother'), siostra ('sister') which are used to address friars and nuns, respectively. At least three other institutionalized forms include: oskarżony/oskarżona ('the accused') and świadek ('witness'), all of which occur in courtroom situations. One can also use other forms (names, diminutives, nick-names, etc.) for indirect address in Polish, but this point need not be pursued further here.

As has been mentioned, the addressing of males is the central focus of Pisarkowa's analysis. This same bias is also present in some other recent works on the address system of Polish by other authors whose work will be mentioned shortly. Treating males as central, and focusing on the language used by and with them, treating females' usage as marginal or simply unimportant is taken here as an indication of (meta)linguistic sexism in the studies of Polish address forms. In order to show that not all of the claims which have been made about the address system of (standard) Polish are equally valid for Polish men and women, I will use, apart from my own intuition, data collected from seven contemporary novels.[7]

What is more striking about some of the studies on the Polish address system is the fact that one of the most important extralinguistic factors determining the choice of an appropriate form of address, i.e., the sex of the addressee (and of the addresser) is not overtly recognized. Zaręba (1981) says that the use of a given form of address, in general, depends on "such factors as the age of the interlocutors, their social statuses, i.e., profession or social function, possible titles and, of course, their mutual relationship" (1981:1).

For Tomiczek (1983), the choice of a particular form of address depends on the profession, age and education of each interlocutor. If Zaręba and Tomiczek had recognized the need to pay more attention to sex-linked differences in address, they would probably have noticed that address by and with women does not exactly follow the rules that hold for men, and that women's address should not be treated as a deviation from a male norm.

In contemporary Polish there are certain professional titles and names for women which originally referred to men and are masculine in gender. These usually refer to occupations and professions that enjoy a high status. When these nominal forms refer to females, they are uninflected (i.e., they remain in the nominative case) even when they appear in a sentence in a non-subject position (cf. Klemensiewicz 1982 [1957]), e.g.,

Rozmawiałem z (panią) profesor.
('I spoke with the [lady] professor.')
Daj to (pani) inżynier.
('Give it to the [lady] engineer.')

The same rule applies when these forms are used as forms of address, where one hears the vocative[8] for addressing a man (e.g., Panie profesorze! ['Mr. Professor!']), the nominative case is used when a woman is the addressee (e.g., Pani profesor! ['Ms. Professor!']). Most nominal vocatives are two-place forms (e.g., Panie doktorze! ['Mr. Doctor!']; Pani doktor! ['Ms. Doctor']) but in some cases the second part of these forms may be used alone as a vocative. Pisarkowa (1979:9-10) says that "such uses emphasize the integration factor, and even that of intimacy: Profesorze! ['Professor!'], Majorze! ['Major!'], Dyrektorze! ['Director!']."[9] However, she does not mention that the three examples she quotes can be used to address males only, which makes forms of this kind sex-specific. It is possible to address a female with an occupational title alone only if this title is morphologically marked as feminine, e.g., kierowniczka ('manager[ess]'), or when it is semantically female, e.g., siostra ('sister'). This results in rendering forms like Kierowniczko! and Siostro! which, again, are sex-specific.

Similar male-centred discussion of the forms in question can be found in Tomiczek (1983). He recognizes the difference in male/female address in forms like panie magistrze vs. pani magister (1983:115) but fails to see the lack of correspondence between the forms magistrze vs. *magister[10] for males and females, respectively.

Women are also made invisible in other ways in studies dealing with Polish forms of address. For example, Pisarkowa's (1979) discussion of the form(s) kolega (koleżanka) is only illustrated with examples pertaining to male to male speech. She says that these forms of address do not allow reciprocation and lists the following examples: kolego ('colleague'), drogi kolego ('dear colleague'), kolego docencie ('colleague docent'), kolego doktorze ('colleague doctor'), and panie kolego ('Mr. colleague'). As mentioned earlier, these forms cannot be treated as generic, and they are interpreted by Polish native speakers as specifically referring to males. There is also a difference in how the titles kolega and koleżanka are used for addressing males and females, respectively. It seems that vocatives with kolega are used with men more often than vocatives with koleżanka are used for females. The least difference probably occurs between these two forms when they are used alone: Kolego!, Koleżanko! In Polish hospitals male doctors tend to receive more forms with kolega from their superiors (i.e., kolego+LN, kolego doktorze, panie kolego); females receive fewer forms with koleżanka. In place of such forms as koleżanko+FN, ?*koleżanko doktor(ze) and ?pani koleżanko, females would more likely receive forms like pani doktor, and pani+FN (whose masculine counterpart are, of course, also available for men), but not *doktor(ze), which, however, is used for men.

In an examination of forms of address used in seven contemporary Polish novels, the difference in the use of kolega and koleżanka as forms of address is clearly apparent. Only in one novel (Broszkiewicz 1981) does koleżanka appear as a form of address, but even then it is not used as a vocative but rather in indirect address. On the other hand, in Bohdziewicz (1981) a male professor addresses his male student as panie kolego ten times in one conversation. In Broszkiewicz (1981) males use forms like kolego, panie kolego, drogi panie kolego ('dear Mr. colleague'), etc. to a great extent. Likewise in Hen (1985) forms like panie kolego and kolego+LN used among males do not have any equivalents with koleżanko when females are addressed.

Similarly, other terms of address expressing camaraderie among men are not paralleled by the feminine forms to the same degree. In Ciapało (1983) bracie ('brother') appears three times among non-kin males, and brachu ('brother') appears once in a letter. In Broszkiewicz (1981) panie bracie ('brother') is also used once between non-kin males. The vocative siostro ('sister') (not in address to kin, nun or nurse) appears twice in Biliński (1983). It is worth mentioning, however, that these two instances of siostro appear in the speech of only one woman (Pola) with her ex-husband's new wife (Sylwia), and therefore it has more of the features of address between members of the same family. Both women are related to each other through the person of one man, which allows them to be treated as members of one family, and they are not on the best terms, which does not suggest an interpretation of the form siostro used by one of them as an expression of camaraderie. Furthermore, in this scene, Pola uses a patronizing tone with Sylwia, much like an older sister talking to her younger, inexperienced sibling.

That kolega and koleżanka are, in different contexts, used non-symmetrically for males and females may also be inferred from the analysis of two other forms whose lexical meanings are similar to those of kolega and koleżanka, namely, przyjaciel and przyjaciółka ('friend'). Zaręba (1981) says that "the word przyjaciel appears in Polish address only occasionally, and exclusively in the written language. Thus today, the forms mój przyjacielu ['my friend'], and drogi przyjacielu ['dear friend'] do not function in spoken Polish at all" (Zaręba 1981:6-7). However, he adds in a footnote that "the form przyjacielu (without the modifiers mój or drogi) functions only in colloquial usage: adult person:boy, for example in the sentence: Słuchaj, przyjacielu, gdzie tu jest poczta? ['Listen friend, where is the post-office here?']" (Zaręba 1981:7, footnote 8).

In my opinion, Zaręba's account of the use of the form(s) przyjacielu (przyjaciółko) is not very accurate. First of all, he has nothing to say on the non-usability of the form przyjaciółko as a form of address with/among women, and, of lesser importance here, he is wrong in saying that the masculine form appears only in the written language (what kind?), as it is still heard among male peers and it is still used by socially superior men to their male subordinates, and not only to young boys. In my literary data, the form przyjacielu appears in one novel (Broszkiewicz 1981) four times in the speech of one adult male to another adult male, but przyjaciółko does not appear as a form of address with a female. A plausible explanation of the fact that przyjaciółko is not used as a form of address is that it has become to mean 'lover', and this connotation is much stronger in this feminine term than in its masculine counterpart.

Stary ('old man') and stara ('old woman') can function as vocatives among peers of both sexes as a mark of camaraderie, implying not the old age of the addressee but probably the fact that the relationship between any two persons exchanging this form has lasted for a long time. Again, males tend to use and receive this form more often than females. In the literary sources reviewed, various men receive this form from other men more than 40 times, but it is never once used with females. This does not mean that females do not ever use and receive this term of address in real life, but it seems that literature reflects in a somewhat extreme way the actual imbalance in the frequency that stary vs. stara is used.

As for more patronizing terms of address, like chłopcze ('boy'), dziewczyno ('girl'), the literary data indicate that adult females receive (usually from males) the form dziewczyno more often than adult males receive chłopcze, and the former is more readily used with sexual overtones (cf. however, chłopczyku used by prostitutes to men).

There exists an even greater contrast between the seemingly parallel forms chłopie ('man'), babo ('woman/you silly woman'). Unlike the former, which is used as yet another term to express camaraderie with males, the latter is clearly an insult.

Of course, there also exist similar terms for men, e.g., dziadu, dziadzie ('you silly old man'), just like a host of other pejorative derivatives of babo for women.

Interestingly enough, one can also insult a man by calling him babo, whereas one cannot successfully insult a woman by calling her chłopie or even dziadu.

One more form of address worthy of mention in this section is based on the word człowiek ('human being'). The word człowiek is, in a number of contexts, a false generic (cf. Chapter 2), and has a strong male bias when it is used referentially. The same bias is preserved when it is used vocatively:

Człowieku! Uważaj co robisz!

(' [Hey] man! Look what you're doing!')

Although one can hear człowieku in utterances directed to women (usually from other women), this is rare compared to the frequency with which men are addressed with this term, and the function of this vocative when used with women is narrower than when it is used to address men. When used to address a woman, człowieku becomes a kind of exclamation that expresses great surprise, awe or some other strong feelings and emotions, as for example, in the following:

Poszliśmy tam i, człowieku, co tam się działo!

('We went there, and, oh man/oh boy, the things that were happening there.')

According to Zwicky (1978) "Vocatives serve at least two functions: they can be calls or addresses" (Zwicky 1978:787). Zwicky illustrates these two functions with the two following examples, the former illustrating a call, the latter an address:

Hey lady, you dropped your piano.

I'm afraid, sir, that my coyote is nibbling on your leg.

Apart from its 'exclamatory' function mentioned earlier, the vocative człowieku can also be used as a call:

Człowieku, wyjdź z tej dziury.

(' [Hey] man, get out of this hole!'),

or it can be used as an address:

Dlaczego, człowieku, nie zostawisz mnie w spokoju?

('Why, man, don't you leave me alone?').

However, in both these functions człowieku is strongly preferred in addressing men; compare:

Człowieku, przestań mnie pan pchać!

(' [Hey] man, stop pushing me, mister!')

*Człowieku, przestań mnie pani pchać!

???(' [Hey] man, stop pushing me, lady!')

Powiedz mi coś, człowieku, o swojej żonie.
('Tell me, man, something about your wife.)
*Powiedz mi coś, człowieku, o swoim mężu.
???('Tell me, man, something about your husband.)

In place of człowieku one would rather say kobieto (or kobito) ('woman') when addressing a woman.

Powiedz mi coś, kobieto, o swoim mężu.
('Tell me, woman, something about your husband.')

On the other hand, mężczyzno ('man' - non-generic) is not used vocatively, except in some limited cases, e.g.,

Mężczyzno mojego życia!
('Your're the man of my life!')

In the seven novels consulted the vocative człowieku appeared in the speech of men and women, but only to address males. This form appeared either alone or with such modifiers as młody ('young'), biedny ('poor'), wielki ('great'), etc. Zaręba (1981) notices the male bias of this vocative but is wrong in saying that it is used only among men (women also use this form with men and sometimes, though rarely, with one another). With regard to człowieku Tomiczek (1983:198) quotes the following example:

CZŁOWIEKU, daj mi PAN wreszcie skończyć!
('Man, let me finish at last!')

but fails to observe that if pani were used instead of pan in the same sentence, it would sound ridiculous to any native speaker of Polish:

*Człowieku, daj mi pani wreszcie skończyć!
???('Man, let me finish at last [lady]!').

Returning to Pisarkowa's (1979) article it is possible to find other examples in her analysis which point to the fact that she has been primarily concerned with Polish address forms used for men rather than both men and women. Pisarkowa presents a chart (pp. 12-13) in which she represents all the possible types of the forms of address which she deals with in her study and the verbal forms with which they co-occur. In the chart, she states that the term obywatel ('citizen') may appear as a form of address with such forms as: prezydent ('president'), minister ('minister'), ambasador ('ambassador'), rektor ('rector'), dziekan ('dean'), dyrektor ('director'), redaktor ('journalist'), szef ('chief/boss'), doktor ('doctor'), etc., and with such academic titles as: profesor, doktor and magister. All these terms combine with obywatel into one form of address, however, with the possible exception of szef, but mostly when they are used with male addressees. The use of these forms with female addressees seems less likely. In other words, while the difference is not a qualitative one, the quantitative difference should be recognized. The term obywatelko for females is largely replaced in actual speech with women by the term pani, for example, pani redaktor ('Ms. journalist'), pani dziekan ('Ms. dean') instead of ?obywatelko redaktor, ?obywatelko dziekan.

Likewise, Pisarkowa's chart implies that the forms prezydent, ambasador, etc. can be used on their own in the vocative case. This is true, of course, but only in regard to male addressees (cf. above).

Finally, Pisarkowa includes in her chart the possibility that the terms prezydent, ambasador, etc., can be used in the genitive or accusative cases with the word proszę ('please') to function as vocatives, e.g., proszę prezydenta, proszę ambasadora, proszę doktora. She does not, however, comment on the fact that proszę does not combine with these terms when a woman is the addressee: *proszę prezydent, *proszę ambasador, *proszę doktor.

To end the discussion of sex-related differences in the use of terms of address in Polish, some forms expressing intended intimacy between the addresser and the addressee should be mentioned. Zaręba (1981) states the following about some of them:

> One form that has recently come to be used more often among women [than among men] is the phrase moja kochana ['my beloved one'] or moja droga ['my dear']. These phrases are widely used in certain social groups, for example, among [female] office clerks, secretaries [...] saleswomen, etc. These forms are sometimes used with strangers or near-strangers, for example, with [female] customers in shops or [female] clients in offices. This is an expression of a type of patronizing attitude (Zaręba 1981:4).

My literary data do not fully confirm this claim. First, these terms are also used among intimates in same and cross-sex dyads. Second, not only distant women but also distant men use them for distant women, and women tend not to reciprocate these forms with distant men. Men do not seem to use these forms among themselves as often as women do. When a man who is on intimate terms with a woman uses one of the 'intimate' forms (otherwise referred here to as 'terms of endearment') of address with her, the address often carries sexual overtones or else it is condescending. A number of other terms of intimacy not mentioned by Zaręba fall into this group, and it turns out that (at least in the novels from which my data come) males, both distant and intimate, have a larger repertoire of such terms for the purpose of addressing women, than women do for the purpose of addressing others.[11] The following list of terms of endearment from five of the seven novels analyzed[12] make this point clear, though it has not been indicated which forms were used between intimate speakers and which were used between distant ones (the figures in brackets indicate the number of occurrences of a given term):

male to male
mój drogi (3) ('my dear')
panie złoty (1) ('golden sir')

female to female
kochana (4) ('beloved')
kochana+FN (1)
kochanie (3) ('darling')
moja droga (1) ('my dear')
złociutka (1) ('you golden one')
złotko ty moje (1) ('you my golden one')
skarbie (1) ('you treasure')

male to female
kochanie (14)
kochana+FN (3)
darling* (2)
miła moja (2) ('my kind one')
mała (3) ('little one')
dziecino (1) ('baby')
moja droga (4)
kitty* (1)
my daughter*/+ (1)
dziecko+ (1) ('child')
córeczko+ (1) ('daughter')
moje dziecko+ (1) ('my child')
droga sąsiadko (1) ('dear neighbour')

female to male
kochany (6) ('beloved')
kochanie (3)
moje dziecko+ (1)
mój drogi (1)
kochaniutki (1) ('beloved')

panie kochany (2) ('beloved sir')

*These forms appeared originally in English.

+These forms were not used between kin.

In this, admittedly limited, corpus of data concerning terms of endearment, 53.8% of all these terms are used by males with females, 21.5% by females with males, 18.5% by females with females, and 6.2% by males with males.

Apart from the researchers' disregard of sex-linked differences in the Polish address system, they also ignore the problem of whether it is the man or the woman that has a right to initiate a shift from formal to informal address. Stone (1981) is the only one who has, to my knowledge, dealt with this problem so far:

> The proposal to drink <u>bruderszaft</u>, i.e., to change to reciprocal T, can only be made in accordance with certain rules of precedence. In the words of Kamyczek's guide to etiquette the proposal can only be made by "the more important person to the less important" (1974:184). Importance is measured mainly in terms of (i) age, (ii) social and professional rank, but in addition women are also considered (despite statements to the contrary, e.g., Kamyczek 1974:177) to have certain superior claims in this matter. This latter fact does not concord with the generalization, based on Brown and Gilman's data, that right to initiate reciprocal T belongs to "the member of the dyad having the better power-based claim to say T without reciprocation" (1972:261) (Stone 1981:69).

Stone's account of the problem of reciprocal shift to informal address within a mixed-sex dyad is slightly confusing. The reader cannot be quite sure if, after all, women have "certain superior claims in this matter" or not. Does Stone believe that a Polish man has "the better power-based claim to say T without reciprocation"? Furthermore, in the paragraph from which Stone quoted only an excerpt, Brown & Gilman conclude that "The suggestion that solidarity be recognized comes more gracefully [...] from the female than from the male" (Brown & Gilman 1972:261).

This does not help clarify Stone's point as to whether women in Polish have a greater power base claim over men in the initiation of address shifts to informal terms.[13]

In the literary sources consulted for the use of address forms in Polish, the actual <u>bruderszaft</u> situations appeared very infrequently. In one such situation (Nowacka 1976:18) it was a woman who suggested it to a man,[14] and she was clearly making a pass at him. This situation is somewhat unusual in that other female characters in this and the other novels are not portrayed as initiating close relations with men; the opposite is more often the case. The fact that men are depicted in the novels as making more passes at women rather than vice versa is also reflected in the men's more frequent initial (without bruderszaft) and continual use (despite the women's lack of reciprocation) of the women's FNs.

In the light of the above discussion, and the data for the American system of address summarized at the beginning of the present chapter, it is possible to draw some general conclusions which, especially for Polish, need further empirical corroboration.

1. Polish and (American) English systems of address reflect definite sex-linked differences in the use of forms of address.

2. The inventories of forms of address used by and with women tend, in both languages, to be smaller than those for men, perhaps with the exception of terms of endearment, of which women receive more in both languages.

3. The patterns of usage for forms of address in Polish and (American) English indicate that, in mixed-sex dyads, men are in control of the situation and dominate women (cf. their larger repertoires of forms of address and their more frequent initiation of informal address with women).

4. The area of address provides further proof that the Polish word człowiek is a false generic, since it is not as commonly used for addressing women as it is for men. This phenomenon is related to the fact that the false English generic man also cannot be used as a form of address for women. (However, consider you guys said to a mixed-sex group or even to an all female one.)

5. Polish and English differ with respect to the use of social titles for women. The former has practically abandoned the use of the form panno ('Miss') with unmarried women. Pani ('Ms.', originally 'Mrs.') is used today for all adult females. On the other hand, the debate of whether to introduce the non-sexist social title for women (Ms.) is still under way in the English-speaking world (cf. Hook 1974).

6. As far as the **studies** of address systems are concerned, they should account for both male and female language use. Likewise, one should not expect to find examples of sexist (meta)language in such studies, as in the following example from Zaręba (1981), where the generic word młodzież ('youth') is used with a male bias:

> Wśród młodzieży można usłyszeć czasem takie zwroty: No co, chłopaki, idzemy? albo wśród dziewcząt: Fajno dziewczyny! (Zaręba 1981:10).

> ('Among youth one can sometimes hear forms like: Well, boys, are we going? or among the girls: Fine, girls!')

A peculiar instance of sexism embedded in the structure of an analysis of Polish and German address systems surfaces in Tomiczek's (1983:186, 190) two diagrams representing address among kin in the two languages. In both diagrams ego is unilaterally linked to other possible family members with arrows. In both cases ego is male, and separate, one-way arrows point to ego's wife. The androcentrism of this example certainly needs no further comment.

Notes

1. However, Pisarkowa (1979:8) says that pan(i) is the most neutral term of address in Polish. I will not take up the issue of neutrality of Polish forms of address here.
2. By indirect address I mean addressing someone in the third person (singular) (e.g., Czy mama przyjdzie? ['Will (you) mom come?']) (see Svennung 1958).
3. A speech community is understood here as a group of people using what can intuitively be defined as one language (e.g., English, Polish, German) to communicate with each other within a given territory.
4. Schubert (1985) quotes a similar example from a Semitic language (Amharic) in which it is polite to address women with the masculine pronoun antɛ, whereas addressing a man with the feminine pronoun anci indicates either a very intimate relationship or an insult.
5. The term 'indirect address' is used to refer to the use of these forms (cf. note 2).
6. Stone (1981) mentions similar problems in the works of others. He says that when Klemensiewicz (1946), Loś (1916), Brückner (1916) and Westfal (1975) discuss the usage of pan, they probably mean to subsume forms like pani under this form in order to account for address of women, and panowie ('gentlemen'), panie ('ladies') and państwo ('ladies and gentlemen'). Perhaps Stone is right, and the researchers he mentions meant to include females in their discussions, but because pan is not a generic word, this is hard to believe.
7. The following literary sources were consulted on the use of forms of address in Polish: Andrzejewski (1981); Ciapało (1983); Broszkiewicz (1981); Bohdziewicz (1981); Biliński (1983); Nowacka (1976); and Hen (1985).
8. The term 'vocative' is used here as a functional category in the sense Zwicky (1974) uses it for English. To distinguish this sense of the term from the 'vocative' as a grammatical category of case, whenever it is used in the latter sense, it will be labelled as 'vocative case'.
9. It may also be mentioned in passing that such uses of titles need not always mark greater integration or intimacy between interlocutors. Sometimes, their use can work quite to the contrary, i.e., when a superior addresses an inferior in this way, the increase of distance may be intended (cf. Jaworski 1982 for a discussion of this type of usage in a military setting).
10. The use of asterisks and question marks before some examples of forms of address indicates not so much their ungrammaticality in the traditional sense of syntactic studies, but rather the high improbability of occurrence of a given form in a given context.
11. The pattern of usage for terms of endearment in Polish seems to match that of American English (cf. McConnell-Ginet 1978:32 quoted earlier in the present chapter).

12. No terms of endearment are listed from Broszkiewicz (1981) and Hen (1985).
13. It is worth noting that Stone is certainly wrong in his description of the act of bruderszaft saying that "the ceremony can only be performed when wine is being drunk (beer or spirits are not acceptable)" (Stone 1981:69). Vodka, of course, is as acceptable (or even more so) as wine for drinking bruderszaft.
14. The beverage drunk on this occasion was Albanian brandy (see footnote 13).

4

Sexism in education:
Foreign language teaching

The present chapter deals with sexism in education, and will specifically focus on sexism in foreign language materials (textbooks) in three sections. First, a review of some of the arguments made by other authors writing on sexism in foreign language materials will be provided with the aim of drawing attention to the need for more objectivity in further research in this area. Then, an analysis of the sexist content of some of the textbooks used in Poland for teaching English will be presented. That is followed by an analysis of the sexist language in these textbooks.

The working definition of sexism adopted here for the study of discrimination against women in education is the same as that used by Hellinger (1980:267):

> Textbooks are sexist if they omit the actions and achievements of women, if they demean women by using patronizing language or if they show women and men only in stereotyped roles with less than the full range of human interests, traits and capabilities (Scott, Foresman and Company 1972:1).

Over the last decade, a number of studies have been published which evaluate foreign language materials in terms of their attitude to the characterization of males and females in various situations, the presentation of male and female roles in target societies, the use of sexist language, etc. In this section some of these issues will be reviewed.

All of the studies that deal with sexism in foreign language materials (henceforth: FLM) that have been consulted for the purpose of this section represent overviews of written materials (textbooks) that have been developed only for the teaching of European languages (predominantly English). Some of them examine only one text (in one or more volumes); others deal with selections from different textbooks and deal with one or more languages. Although the studies of women's roles in the FLM used here differ in their respective treatments of sexism, they generally agree with other analyses of this kind that deal with sexism in the mass-media and in other areas of education, and they point to similar, and sometimes identical problems.[1] Rickel & Grant's (1979) study, based on the individual analyses of other authors, summarizes the prevailing types of sexism in American mass-media and education; these largely fit the picture of sexism in FLM:

> 1. different occupational roles for men and women, 2. underrepresentation of women and overrepresentation of men, 3. women in the roles of victims, butts of jokes, targets of insults, and makers of self-depreciating remarks, 4. different modes of achievement in men and women, and 5. trivialization of women and their concerns (Rickel & Grant 1979:165).

One more point may be added to the above in order to complete the picture of sexism described in studies dealing with FLM, namely, the stereotyping of women and, to a lesser degree, men. Perhaps this sixth point need not be listed separately since it underlies all the others (with the exception of 2).

The studies consulted here do not emphasize all five points to the same degree. It is difficult, at this point, to provide a definite characterization of the differences that occur in the textbooks designed for teaching particular languages, or produced in particular countries. However, certain differences may be pointed out in the way sexist issues are presented in different textbooks, and how certain critics perceive them.

For example, Bressan (1978), speaking of an Italian grammar text, stresses "the underlying machismo [...] characterizing 'Italiano Vivo's' attitudes to women in society" (1978:31), and he quotes numerous examples of sexism in the textbook's description of marriage and other male-female relations. Analyzing an American text for the teaching of English, Carroll (1978) emphasizes the perpetuation of the stereotype of a single woman desperately looking for a husband, and the importance of a woman's beauty: the basic virtue necessary to make others (mostly men) appreciate her. Textbooks for teaching Polish make especially numerous references to their female characters' often being late (Jaworski 1983), suggesting that Poles may be especially preoccupied with the importance of clock time in general.[2]

Naturally, these and other themes are common for most of these studies regardless of the target language of the textbook or its place of origin. This may indicate that differences in the ways sexism manifests itself in FLM (when present) are quantitative rather than qualitative.

The following discussion will analyze some of the arguments for treating certain FLM as sexist, which should make clear that sexism is a complex problem, and that theoretical and practical problems arise when studies of sexism in FLM are considered.

Grandcolas (1978) complains that an English textbook underrepresents women by presenting them in too few job situations, and she adds that

> as soon as a woman is not a housewife, she has either a very traditional job (she is a nurse or a teacher) or a most unusual occupation (novelist, spy or ... witch). We never see a woman working in an office, driving a taxi or graduating as a doctor (Grandcolas 1978:69).

It is not hard to agree that women should be presented in more than five (six including 'housewife') occupations in one textbook, but the complaint that some of the professions mentioned above are too "usual" or "unusual" seems not to be a valid one. The textbook representing women in a limited range of professions is sexist because it overshadows the actual role of women in society, and any small number of women depicted in the world of professional careers incurs the risk of tokenism on the one hand, and stereotyping on the other.

What if the textbook analyzed by Grandcolas portrayed women in two other professions: as secretaries and taxi-drivers? It would not be very hard to indicate that the image of a woman "working in an office" could be as sexist as its absence in a textbook. As for the second profession, it seems that though there are some female taxi-drivers, at least in Poland, this is still considered a rather unusual job for a woman. Besides, one may wonder why the professions of spy and novelist in FLM should be considered unsuitable for women. Finally, the omission of women in the characterizations of professions that are dominated by them in reality (e.g., elementary school teachers) may be even more sexist than simply limiting them to these most "usual" occupations (cf. p. 75).

Ittzés (1978) gives several examples of the unfortunate depiction of girls in comparison to boys in a Hungarian four-volume, high-school textbook for English. The author states that, in the textbook descriptions, girls talk less frequently than boys, have fewer interests, participate in fewer social events (in fact, only one), etc. A birthday party involving some girls is also said to embody sexist elements:

> We are also informed that "They laughed a lot at Peggy's jokes". Yes, the role of the clown must also be played by a girl (Ittzés 1978:21).

It is surprising that joke telling by a female should bring such an interpretation.

Humorous and witty performance seems to be a highly valued skill in many societies, though I have no data available on the status of joke-tellers in Hungary. It also seems that other authors of articles on sexism in FLM would not mind seeing females depicted as joke or story-tellers in the textbooks they review. Stern (1976), for example, describes a male character from a French textbook whose positive features include the following:

> He is nice; he is friendly; he likes jokes and gay songs. He is a natural storyteller with his southern accent (Stern 1976:269).

Even the word clown acquires a positive connotation when it is used in reference to males; Hartman & Judd (1978) mention some boys in one textbook as being freer to do more than girls as they are also shown "clowning in the classroom" (Hartman & Judd 1978:387).

What is done in FLM by males is usually said to be good (for them) and reflecting their positive and dominant position in society. What is done by females evokes opposite associations. When males and females do the same or very similar things in different textbooks, their activities may acquire different ratings on the scale of sexism from those who study the subject.

Ittzés mentions the fact that

> boys [...] never, in all four books, go shopping or help their mothers in any other way. But no, they do enter some shops. There is a story in pictures about Tom who loses his money. Can you see where he is going? (Ittzés 1978:21).

Yes, we can. He is going to a sweet shop, as the reproduced illustration shows. Now, imagine that this story is about a girl. It would be very easy to show that the picture story is sexist. First, we could object to the fact that **she** goes shopping again, even though girls always help their mothers with shopping. Secondly, the idea of wasting money would acquire a sexist connotation: when boys waste their money on sweets, it is because they are independent; when girls do the same it is regarded as one of their faults. An example of the latter is provided by Gaff (1982). The author speaks of a biased presentation of a girl in a French textbook: "she spends all her pocket-money on sweets [...] and cannot understand why she has a toothache" (Gaff 1982:74).

Although in different studies there are not too many contradictory statements about what is and what is not sexist in FLM, some of the arguments seem to be easily refuted.

Sartori Stein (1978) says that women in the FLM she has examined are "seen as sprendthrifts [sic] or as gambling away money" (Sartori Stein 1978:131). Among the five examples she uses to illustrate her point is this one from a German text:

> Frau Meyer hat tausend Mark im Kasino verloren, und Meyer hat sich furchtbar darüber aufgeregt" (Sartori Stein 1978:131).

The implication of the above text is that the female has wastefully lost her (her husband's?) money, and that her husband is concerned. Think of a reverse situation. In such a case one might object to the fact that only males have the right to gamble their money away, but their fun is, inevitably, spoiled by their nagging wives.

Gaff (1982) presents us with the picture of a girl (Marie-Claude) from a French textbook which she considers sexist. The girl is said to be shown in the textbook as a negative character in comparison with her brothers, who are said to be good characters.

> Her faults are many: she cheats at school and at cards [...] she spends all her pocket-money on sweets (the boys save a proportion of theirs) and cannot understand why she has a toothache [...] she inflicts noisy TV programmes featuring appalling pop-singers on the rest of the family [...] she takes and rides away a horse from the riding school without permission, and is justly punished by falling and breaking her arm [...] and she is rude to Philippe's English pen-pal, making disparaging remarks about boys in general, and is again justly punished, this time by being pushed into a ditch at the zoo. When Mme Bertillon is injured riding her moped and has to spend a few days in hospital [...] Marie-Claude of course takes over her mother's role in the house; but she shirks her share of the work, bosses the others about, and unjustly takes all the credit for their work on Mme Bertillon's return" (Gaff 1982:74).

The picture of Marie-Claude that the reader gets is definitely not a positive one. Marie-Claude is, however, very much different from most other girls depicted in the FLM examined by authors of other studies of sexism. At least some of the things which Marie-Claude does are not "naturally" feminine and, in contrast to other textbooks, they are not done by males. She is not one of the obedient, lady-like, always submissive to the male authority, stereotypical girls, reported in other studies. Consider the following quote:

> And it seems boys do well if they rely on girls. The girls do anything for them without complaint (Ittzés 1978:20).

Marie-Claude will not do anything for anybody without complaint.

That women "show a limited number of human traits: helplessness, fear, loneliness, worry, avarice: but never anger, aggression, or ambition (except for marriage)" (Carroll 1978:59), is regarded, and quite rightly so, as a sign of sexism embodied in an English textbook. However, one has to admit that Marie-Claude is sometimes angry and aggressive, too.

She is at least one girl who does not want to please others around her (e.g., she chooses the TV programmes **she** wants to watch). She is physically active and loves horseback riding (if her brother were the horse lover, it might be considered "natural" that it is a boy who takes to sports). She is untypically unfeminine when she makes rude remarks of men; most other studies quote insulting remarks made by men and directed at women. Even Gaff herself quotes Marie-Claude's brother insulting her (1982:75), which, needless to say, is considered sexist. Marie-Claude is pushed into a ditch - if she had done the pushing, this would just provide further proof that she is the nasty one. Finally, she is at least one girl who bosses others about. Had she dutifully done all the housework, she would only have conformed to the common stereotype of a helpful daughter.

Other authors who have written about sexism in FLM think that it is sexist to have to read only about sons who are disobedient, a pattern that reinforces the stereotype of passive and dull daughters who present no disciplinary problems (cf. Grancolas 1978:68).

One may wonder if the examples of sexism in FLM provided by some studies are even appropriate. Sometimes, it seems that a passage almost automatically gets a sexist label if it simply deals with women.

> The jokes do not put women in a better light. Women appear as scatterbrained or flimsy; old women are not better served:
> "Why did it take three boys to help the little old lady across the street? She did not want to go" (Grandcolas 1978:71).

It is not easy to agree that the joke quoted above is, in any special way, targeted against women. For an international audience the same joke works and appears to be equally funny when "old lady" is replaced by "old man". It seems that the funniness of the joke lies not in the fact that it ridicules anyone, but in the humorous situation itself. As a matter of fact, this type of humour (i.e., situational) may suit women even more than men, who seem to prefer a verbal, more aggressive type of humour (cf. Kramarae 1981:61).

One author (Sartori Stein 1978) provides examples from various textbooks that express the opinion that a woman's only goal is to get married. Two of the examples quoted in her article, however, seem to be either non-sexist or sexist to both men and women:

> She isn't married. She's still a single woman.
> He isn't married. He's single and he lives alone. (1978:127)
>
> We told the American soldier to marry a French girl. (1978:128)

If one looks at FLM in this way, anything can work against females. Ittzés speaks twice about the types of presents males and females give for birthdays:

> Even their [girls'] presents show that they are given by girls: "Everyone gave Joe a present. John gave him a fountain-pen, Tom brought him a book. Peggy bought him three handkerchiefs, Katie a record and some sweets' [...] Which boy would think of buying sweets or handkerchiefs for Joe? They are more serious than that (Ittzés 1978:21).

However, when the boy's father gives his son something "less serious" it is still better than the mother's gift:

> When Joe is sixteen, his mother presents him with a "beautiful birthday cake" [...] His father's present, though small, is more manly: a tie (Ittzés: 1978:18).

In most studies of sexism in FLM, considerably little time and space is devoted to the problem of discrimination against men. As a matter of fact, one would not find any textbook that actually underrepresents males, as the reverse (i.e., the overrepresentation of males) is true. However, in many texts men are also stereotyped and this is just as unfair as the stereotyping of women.

This problem is recognized by Hartman & Judd (1978), who state: "Aside from omission [of women] the most pervasive sexism we noted is the shunting of women and men into stereotypical roles" (1978:385). They also give several examples of the stereotyping of both sexes. Murdoch & Murdoch (1978) acknowledge the stereotyping of the central character in a German textbook written in Britain, but they suggest that "he presents the dominant stereotype role" (Murdoch & Murdoch 1978:89). Dominant need not imply positive, however. And in a few other papers (Ittzés 1978; Rees-Parnall 1978; Bressan 1978) one finds descriptions of male characters from some textbooks, whose dominance over women approaches misogyny. Unfortunately, this negative stereotyping is not always commented on by those who write about sexism.

The present argumentation is also intended to warn those who write about sexism in FLM not to consider every single sentence about women as sexist. One should also avoid accusing textbooks of sexism on false or quite imaginary grounds. For example, Hill (1980), in her otherwise valuable survey, implies that Rowlands' (1979) textbook is sexist because it

> starts with great promises as the reader is introduced to two management trainees, David and Sheila. However, whilst David goes on to have conversations with a printer and the Personnel Manager, Sheila - after one (apparently fatal!) lunchtime conversation with David - disappears into oblivion (Hill 1980:2).

This description is not true, and the order of events differs from that in the book. First, David's "conversation" with the printer is a simple telephone call in which he inquires about delayed proofs (Unit 5). In the next unit, David and Sheila have lunch in the canteen, and there is nothing fatal about it for Sheila. The conversation with the Personnel Manager takes place in Unit 9, and both David and Sheila appear in Units 7 and 8. Finally, both trainees participate in the conversation with the Personnel Manager, after which Sheila does not disappear into oblivion. In the remaining 34 units of the book following the conversation with David over lunch, she takes part in 21 dialogues (units), whereas David appears only 16 times.

The aim of the above discussion has not been to underestimate the importance of the arguments of those who have tried (on the whole, quite successfully) to identify sexism in FLM. My point has been to show that we may sometimes differ in our opinions as to what should be considered sexist. The observed differences may result from the cultural differences and personal experiences of the authors of the studies considered here, although still too little evidence is available to decide if there are any definite cross-cultural differences in how sexism is reinforced in FLM.

Finally, I would also propose that studies of sexism, like those quoted above (and the one included in the following section of this chapter), should consider the implications of using some arguments more carefully in order to minimize possible contradictions (or explain the seeming ones) resulting from the use of impressionistic judgements in evaluating FLM.[3]

The following section will deal with sexism present in educational materials, and specifically, some randomly selected Polish textbooks for teaching English as a foreign language (Marton, Lebelt & Grochowska 1976; Michalska & Beven-Oyrzanowka 1977; Mikulska 1980; Smólska & Zawadzka 1969, 1970, 1973a, 1973b; Szkutnik 1979a, 1979b, 1980a, 1980b).

I do not intend to make any evaluative judgements about the pedagogical value of the above-mentioned texts. The only issue here is the sharp contrast in the characterization of men and women in these textbooks and the possible effects this may have on the perception and thought of the students who use them.

Sexism in the textbooks examined here is present in various forms and can be grouped under three categories: omission of women, negative stereotyping of women, and negative contrast with men.

In the numerous dialogues and narrative passages women and men are assigned various roles which should, in order to be accurate, reflect the roles women and men play in real life. In reality not only do a lot of women perform many jobs which used to be the sole domain of males in the past, but women perform them equally well. In the English texts, however, one does not see this change reflected adequately. The number of professions assigned to men is far greater than that assigned to women. Males appear to dominate in almost all professional fields, and they perform more varied, interesting and prestigious jobs including those of astronaut, film director, composer, astronomer, lawyer, sculptor, test pilot, writer, philosopher, medical doctor, teacher, chair of a university department, engineer, linguist, executive, and many others. Apart from a few exceptions which will be mentioned later, women in the English textbooks perform rather inferior, dull and far less numerous jobs than men. The very few jobs reserved solely for women are: dress-maker, nurse, flight attendant, model and, of course, typist, secretary and housewife.

The underrepresentation of women in other professions is appalling. Take, for example, the textbook for children by Michalska & Beven-Oyrzanowska (1977), illustrated by J. Flisak, in which there are pictures of twelve teachers of whom only one is a woman! The only other two jobs women have in this textbook are housewife and cook while men are pictured as cooks, teachers, sailors, doctors and salespersons. Children learning English from a different text (Mikulska 1980), illustrated by A. Kilian, will not be presented with a much better picture of women in the world of professions. Here, women are shown in only seven professions, whereas men are depicted in fifteen.

In all four volumes by Smólska & Zawadzka, doctors invariably appear as male characters, with one notable exception. There is one female doctor mentioned in one book, and she is described by her male colleague: "She is not at all pretty but very intelligent" (1973b:83), and "I think she has a great future before her. A mannish type, not very attractive to men, but a first-class brain" (1973b:146). The perpetuation of the stereotype that beauty and intelligence do not go hand in hand in one woman, in this case a doctor, is not only offensive to all the intelligent and beautiful women who are doctors, but to their dear ones as well.

A similar, though expressed differently, stereotype is found in the same book when we read about Maureen, a model: "She had a lovely figure and a cheerful, rather silly face" (Smólska & Zawadzka 1973b:29).

Smólska & Zawadzka try to make up for their gross exclusion of women from the professional world in only one text: "Looking ahead" (1969:261-262), where Susan and Betty, members of the editorial board for their school magazine, are reading letters from women who have graduated from their school. The stereotyping of women's professions is only slightly reduced here, and the women's professions include a physicist, a flight officer, a flight attendant, and a student of Russian who also "was one of the ten finalists in the Miss Student Britain 1967 contest" (1969:262). One is left to wonder here if the last woman mentioned was really a particularly bright one.

In one textbook, which "is primarily intended for scientists" (Marton et al. 1976:19), not one woman appearing in any of the 69 dialogues in the book is a scientist. There is a Professor Davidson whose sex is not specified and who appears in one dialogue (p. 267), but this does not solve the problem of the male dominance of the book's character. In the numerous exercises in the same book, where women appear as almost nothing other than typists and secretaries, one can also find a few exceptional sentences like: "It is possible that Miss Jane Brown is a scientist" (Marton et al. 1976:41).

The situation in the English textbooks is slightly better as far as the prospective careers of the younger generation are concerned. Both girls and boys want to go to universities and do important things in life. One can, for example, find sentences like: "After graduating Monica wants to be a research worker in microbiology" (Szkutnik 1979a:172). However, the ambitions of boys and girls are also stereotyped to a great extent; boys are given wider areas of interest and some of the young people express their doubts as to whether women should really follow professional careers at all.

The perpetuated stereotype is that boys are better suited than girls for the 'hard' sciences, mathematics and engineering. Consider the following examples:

>   His favourite subject is physics.
>   Her favourite subject is history. (Szkutnik 1979a:16)

>   [...] when I talk to my sister about mathematics, she never understands anything (Szkutnik 1980b:75).

The following example shows another stereotyped view of boys' and girls' interests, together with a stress on male superiority in the area of using one's brains and the 'typically' feminine trait of indecisiveness:

> Paul took eight "O" levels last summer and not only passed them all but got credits in maths, chemistry, and physics. He wants to study physics at Cambridge when he leaves school [...]
> Susan will take her "O" levels this summer. She is quite worried about them. [...] Art, English and geography are her best subjects and she will certainly take them, but what about the other three? She hates chemistry, she is not very good at maths and physics [...] Well, perhaps Paul could help her with her maths [...] Susan will have to ask him when he comes to see her tomorrow (Smólska & Zawadzka 1969:202-203).

Reinforcing stereotypes as in the case illustrated above, is not solely a Polish problem and can be found, along with many of the other issues dealt with here, in a broader cross-cultural perspective. Taking an example from popular press (Johnson 1983) giving a brief account of the situation in Canada, where girls are not encouraged to develop computer skills as much as boys are, shows that this may inhibit girls' success in future search for jobs since they

> will be forced to enter low-paying jobs, many of which will be phased out within the next decade. Indeed, by 1990 most jobs will require some computer skills. Apprenticed in the agressive, poolroom atmosphere of video arcades, the boys have staked out the computer terminal as yet another male preserve (Johnson 1983:45).

The young characters of the English textbooks examined here are not totally insensitive to the problems concerning the position of women in society and their possible emancipation. However, a closer examination of the passages dealing with this topic shows that even here there is room for stereotyping.

In one book (Szkutnik 1980a) one can read that Ann and Monica have totally different ideas about the role of women in society. The former believes that women should stay at home and look after children, while the latter says that women may be married, but should also have interesting jobs. There would be nothing wrong with this text, which after all reflects some girls' ambitions to be good wives and mothers, as well as the ambitions of other girls who may expect something else from life, if not for the illustration accompanying the text (Szkutnik's books are illustrated by W. Andrzejewski). The picture shows two women sitting in rocking chairs. The "traditional" one is knitting, while the "progressive" one is reading The Times and has a lit cigarette in her mouth. This makes the latter character look ridiculous since she is presented in a stereotypically male pose. Furthermore what she is doing is not very creative and is not in accord with the ambitions expressed in the text by the girl with professional interests.

Once Susan (mentioned above) discusses the problem of women's work with her mother (Smólska & Zawadzka 1973a:49-50). She had discussed this problem on the previous day at a meeting of the Debating Society at her school. Susan is full of doubts, since not all of her friends agreed with her that women should not devote "all their time to housekeeping and bringing up the children" (1973a:49). Her mother agrees that while it may be interesting for a woman to have a job, it is very difficult for her to have both a family and a job, so she advises Susan to learn some housekeeping. Susan turns this suggestion down, maintaining that housekeeping is very boring, and asks her mother if she has not heard of "on-the-job training."

There are at least two objections one may raise in connection with this story. First, there is no mention, on either side, of husbands sharing the burdens of the housework. Second, this conversation shows a great inconsistency on the part of the authors who, over and over again, present Susan (but neither of her two brothers) helping Mrs. Wilson with the housework. Only once does Peter, the younger brother, help his mother with Susan, and that is when Mrs. Wilson is sick. Naturally, as a male "unsuited" for housework, Peter ruins Susan's blouse while helping with ironing. On a different occasion, Aunt Helen visits the Wilsons (Smólska & Zawadzka 1970:109), and when she enters the house and finds out from Peter that Susan is studying French in her room, she says: "It's a pity she isn't helping her mother." However, she does not say the same about Peter, who is doing nothing at that moment, or about Robert (the elder brother), who is studying in his room just like Susan.

On the whole, the males in the English textbooks have more fun than females. Daughters help their mothers with the housework and shopping. Boys can play during this time (cf. Mikulska 1980, Book 1&2:70). Boys only help their fathers fix and wash their cars. Fathers take their sons to the lake for a swim, where they also eat food prepared for them by their mothers (Smólska & Zawadzka 1969:240-241). Fathers take their sons to Paris (Szkutnik 1980a:142) and to the Lake District (Szkutnik 1979a:140). When Robert, Philip, Joan and her (unnamed!) sister go on holidays, "The girls do the cooking" (Smólska & Zawadzka 1970:242). When the Wilsons go on holidays, "Mrs. Wilson does the cooking" (ibid.).

In the English textbooks men do not buy food, do not wash, iron or repair their clothes, only occasionally wash the dishes, do not clean up their homes (sometimes they clean their rooms), do not cook, and do not go to the cleaner's. This is how children are introduced to the days of the week in Michalska & Beven-Oyrzanowska (1977; Part 2:10-11):

> On Monday Mother washes Jimmy's trousers, Betty's dress and socks.
> On Tuesday Mother irons and sews.
> On Wednesday Mother cleans the windows.
> On Thursday Mother cleans all the rooms very well. Betty helps her.
> On Friday Mother makes cakes.
> On Saturday Mother goes shopping.
> On Sunday Father does not go to work. Jimmy does not go to school.

One of the few domains of exclusively male activity outside of professional work is driving a car. Men have cars which they are fond of, and they drive them very well. Sometimes, their wives and sisters learn how to drive but are never as good as men. There are two cartoons in Szkutnik's books (1979b:203; 1980b:38) which show women drivers causing car accidents. One of them reinforces another stereotype of women as being too talkative: the driver does not notice that she has run into a lamppost and says to her passenger: "Driving never prevents me from talking."

Women are also shown in other stereotyped situations or are ascribed different negative qualities not shared by men. Following are just a few examples.

1. <u>Women are suspicious.</u> A man is reporting a burglary to a police officer and says about his wife that she "has always been very suspicious of my lonely weekends in this house [...]" (Marton et al. 1976:261).

2. <u>Women are indecisive.</u>

> Jill does not know where she would like to spend her summer holidays. [...] Jill's parents say they would like her to know what their daughter really wants. Unless she tells them now, they will make her plans for her (Szkutnik 1979b:169)

> Oh, Isabel, you're changing your mind again! I've asked you so many times to be more decisive, <u>to think</u> before making decisions. You always make up your mind without thinking - and then you change it a minute later [...]" (Marton et al. 1976:337).

3. <u>Women are emotional.</u>

> It was only then that Dora stopped being sensible and started to cry [...]" (Smólska & Zawadzka 1973a:65).

4. <u>Women worry.</u> In Smólska & Zawadzka (1970:219), there is a whole text about Mrs. Wilson's worries. Elsewhere, Mrs. Wilson is worried about her children, and her

husband gives her advice on what **she** should do to improve their children's conduct.

5. <u>Wives are a pain.</u> In one textbook the reader finds a dialogue in which A interviews B about B's living standards:

> B: Yes, I think I am satisfied [...] But my wife isn't. She's never satisfied.
> A: Why not?
> B: She always wants to have more and more and more ... She keeps saying that I don't earn enough, I'm not ambitious enough, I'm a good-for-nothing ...
> A: Does she work herself? I mean, has she got a job?
> B: No, she hasn't. She's got enough work at home. In fact she spends most of her time at home. That's probably why she wants to have that colour TV set.
> A: She says she wants to have a colour TV set?
> B: Does she say it? Goodness me! She shouts it! (Szkutnik 1980:121-122).

6. <u>Women are trivial.</u> In one dialogue (Marton 1976:274-275), George (the husband) loses his temper while working on an important paper (women never work on papers) after Daisy (the wife) remarks that it is terribly boring and continually interrupts him with all kinds of trivial questions: will he buy her a mink coat? will they talk about their vacation plans? will they go to the party at the Jonses? has he forgotten to buy her a new cocktail dress? Finally, George threatens to kill her and she gets hysterical.

Women are presented in a trivial way even if they have jobs outside their homes. In one dialogue (Marton et al. 1976:178-179), Miss Taylor, who has applied for a secretarial position, explains to the Personnel Manager why she was fired from the firm where she was previously employed:

> [...] there were several steps near my desk at National. Sometimes the male customers fell down these steps. My boss said they fell because I was wearing a miniskirt. He said they weren't watching the steps. Last week a man broke his leg. Then my boss let me go.

7. <u>Men know better.</u> In Smólska & Zawadzka's books, Susan has to admit Paul's superiority at least twice:

> Oh, thanks. "The ABC of Cybernetics." Can you really understand all these things, Paul? That's awfully clever of you. I'm afraid I'll find this book very difficult (Smólska & Zawadzka 1969:213).
>
> "Paul always knows everything," thought Susan not without irritation (Smólska & Zawadzka 1973b:118).

8. Females are forgetful. The two most forgetful (and untidy) people are Stella and Maureen, who share a room in Dulwich (Smólska & Zawadzka 1973b). In a dialogue in Marton et al. (1976:66), two women lose their chemistry books on the same day.

One of the most blatant forms of sexism in the textbooks is the omission of women. The most revealing in this case is the textbook by Marton et al. (1976), where, in a total of 69 dialogues, the proportion of male to female characters is more than 5 to 1; 98 males and only 18 females take part in the dialogues. There are nine dialogues between two speakers whose sex is not specified, 42 dialogues between males only, three dialogues between females, and ten between males and females. There are only five dialogues in which the sex of the speakers is not specified (Dr. Brown, Personnel Manager, Dr. Crank, Prof. Davidson, The Boss, Agent 044).

Similar proportions (6 males to 1 female) occur for the number of male and female characters featured in the illustrations of Szkutnik's textbooks. Another example of the omission of females is a reading passage "On a cattle farm" (Smólska & Zawadzka 1969:135). The characters of this story are introduced in the following way:

> The Hammonds have a cattle farm near Cambridge. [...] Uncle Jim is a very good farmer and his son Jack [...] is interested in farming, too.

The only mention of a female in this text is that of Petunia, Jack's cow.

When women are introduced in the reading passages and dialogues, they are often identified in relation to other male characters and/or defined in terms of their looks and social, but not professional qualities:

Dr. Wilson [...] is a very good doctor.
Mrs. Wilson [...] is a very pleasant woman. (Smólska & Zawadzka 1970:16)

Alec is a shepherd and lives in the cottage together with his wife and two children (Szkutnik 1980a:137).

> Hamlet Weaver has just got back from Heidelberg, West Germany, where he studied philosophy. He specialized in contemporary existentialism (Szkutnik 1980:23).

> Hamlet's girlfriend, Ophelia, is a sweet girl with blond hair. She comes from a middle class family and is rather sentimental. Hamlet finds it rather difficult to talk to her about existentialism, but he likes listening to her singing [...] (Szkutnik 1980:31-32).

One more example of the omission of women is a reading passage in one textbook. This example is very significant in that it indicates how the original sources from which textbook material is gleaned also tend to disregard women. A fragment of Szkutnik's story about the Stone Age era follows:

> The first pictures known to us were made in the Stone Age, some 20,000 years ago. In those days people lived in caves and depended mainly on hunting for their food as they had not yet learned how to farm or keep cattle. When the hunting had not been good, they had to go hungry. As hunting was not easy in those days, men had to make great efforts to keep themselves and their families alive (Szkutnik 1979b:149-150).

The text says that it was the task of the males to hunt in the Stone Age, and this seems to be true. Anthropological sources confirm this fact, and also provide interesting explanations as to why women were and are not often found among the hunters of the hunting-gathering societies (see Dobkin de Rios 1978). However, to say that hunting was the main source of food for these societies is a reflection of the sexist tendency present in some scholarly writings on human prehistory (cf. Chapter 2). What is missing in the above-quoted text is any mention of the role of women in providing food for their families. Tanner (1981:28) comments on this frequently neglected role:

> Female behavior and the behavior of the young [...] were, until this last quarter of the twentieth century, largely neglected. Women's reproductive role, of course, had been acknowledged, but their part in subsistence, protection, play, communication, and tool-making had been ignored. Gathering plants for subsistence, an activity far more certain of result than predation on or hunting of animals, is of such basic importance in the food quest that it is simply amazing that there has been so little inquiry into its invention, development, and effects for the evolving hominids. One thing seems clear: Plant gathering was and is an arena in which females exercised their ingenuity and expended their energy.

Considerably more examples of sexism found in the textbooks examined here could be given. Hopefully, what has already been presented will help to increase awareness, tolerance and understanding of these problems among those concerned with the area of applied linguistics. The totality of the sexist problems has to be dealt with in order to eradicate it from foreign language teaching. It is possible, for example, to cite one textbook where a male and a female are presented on seemingly equal terms, yet, because of the whole context of the textbook, the passage about the female may be considered sexist, while the one about the male may be found neutral.

Szkutnik & Pankhurst (1981a, 1981b, 1981c) include in their textbook one section in which a man speaks of himself in self-demeaning terms, and another in which a woman does so. While the former is a dialogue, and the latter a monologue, this is only a minor difference between the two texts.[4] The dialogue in which the man criticizes himself is just one of many situations in the book in which males appear. The reader encounters far more males in the whole text than females, a clear case of the overrepresentation of males and the underrepresentation of females. The woman's self-depreciating monologue is the only one delivered by a female, although these three volumes contain many such monologues by various men on personal experiences, art, sports, history, etc. (There is one monologue by a Professor Brown whose sex is not specified.) In this context the self-deprecating man is to be taken as a token, or just one of many types of males represented in the text. The woman, however, as the only representative of her sex in all the monologues, instantly becomes a type (cf. Bidwell 1978:44-45).

The last section of the present chapter will deal with another aspect of sexism which is seldom mentioned in the studies of sexism in FLM, namely, the teaching of what is generally considered sexist language, and the use of sexist language and imagery in instructions and explanations of the exercises and grammar sections.

Among the studies of sexism in FLM available to me, only Hartman & Judd (1978:388-390) discuss at any length the sex bias of English in the textbooks they have reviewed. They mention several problems of sexist usage among which the most important are the following:

1. use of generic man/he

2. use of girl to refer to women in contexts when boy is not used to refer to men;

3. weak tendency to signal the title Ms. as an option among the titles available for females;

4. use of more full or titled names for males compared with more first names for females.

A comparison of some textbooks for teaching English and Polish (all published in Poland) adds some new observations to these points.

Polish textbooks for teaching English make use of the masculine generics man and he. From personal teaching experience I know that Polish learners of English, even at the intermediate level, have some problems identifying and/or accepting the masculine gender forms in English as the generic ones.[5] Therefore, one might expect that the use of generic man/he in the following text, especially when the beginning sentence is a contrastive one and it refers to women, will evoke male imagery for the students reading it:

> JAMES'S REFLECTIONS. Modesty is a concept that used to be associated with women. Today, in a slightly different sense, modesty is also associated with academics. For a man to be a good scientist there are important attributes that he must have beyond the purely academic qualities, or so it would seem. He must not only be successful but must apparently be respected or even liked by his colleagues. [...] (Szkutnik & Pankhurst 1981b: 102-103).

In another volume of their textbook, Szkutnik & Pankhurst (1981a) mention the generic man when they explain article usage in English:

> Wyjątek stanowi wyraz m a n (człowiek jako przedstawiciel gatunku), który w tym znaczeniu występuje bez przedimka, np.:
>   Man is mortal   Człowiek jest śmiertelny. (1981a:194)
> ('The exception is the word m a n [human being, representative of the species], which in this meaning appears without any article, e.g., Man is mortal.')

Having learnt the expression "Man is mortal" the Polish learner may want to complete the famous syllogism the way that is possible in Polish, but, as Miller (1983:174) observes, not in English. Compare:

> Men are mortal.   Człowiek jest śmiertelny.
> *Sophia is a man.   Zofia jest człowiekiem.
> ?Sophia is mortal.   Zofia jest śmiertelna.

It may also come as no surprise that in this textbook, in which there are 138 illustrations of males and only 19 illustrations depicting females (and one showing a pair of female legs, [1981b:182]), the following text is illustrated with a picture of a male, though at least some uses of man in this text are supposedly generic:

> This is a man.
> Man is placed in a four-dimensional world.
> He is placed in space which is three-dimensional and in time.
> [...]
> A man receives impressions of the outside world through five main channels.
> He perceives the world through the five main senses (Szkutnik & Pankhurst 1981a:156).

It happens very rarely that non-sexist generics are used in Polish textbooks for English. One instance of the use of such an option is found in Szkutnik & Pankhurst

(1981a:156) in the sentence: "Everyone must accept full responsibility for his or her own life [...]". This sentence appears at the end of a unit featuring a story about a female who says her father "Thought there was something odd with me doing physics - simply because I'm a girl" (1981a:154). The whole text is about the girl's interest in physics and the problems she had to face in order to be able to study it. It seems, then, that if there were more female characters in the textbook, the truly generic pronouns (e.g., he or she) would be used more often. However, since most of the characters are male, the authors of the textbook may have seen no need to include females in the grammar of their 'auxiliary texts' as they did it after the passage in which a female actually appeared.

Similarly, one can find some inconsistency in the use of the generic pronouns in the instructions for the exercises in Marton et al. (1976). In most cases, the students read the instructions suggesting that they are all male, e.g.,

> Make a conversation with another student about his car, television, radio, camera, etc. based on the dialogue (1976:199).

However, the unit which deals with such matters as getting married is followed by an exercise with a different generic pronoun usage:

> Make a conversation with another student about his/her friends, asking him/her questions with comparative constructions (1976:218).

Some Polish used in the textbooks for English discussed here also reveals sexist usage. In each unit of Szkutnik & Pankhurst there is a set of short dialogues in English accompanied by Polish translations. In many cases, when it is not possible to distinguish the sex of the speakers and their interlocutors reading the English versions (the speakers are always marked "A" and "B"), the Polish tranlations reveal that such forms as you, I am sure, etc. stand invariably (with one exception in one dialogue) for males, as they are translated into masculine forms, which, in this context, cannot be "generically" interpreted, and are gender specific.[7]

Likewise, after a dialogue between two males where the phrase "What can I do for you" is introduced, the "Vocabulary study" tells the students that the expression means: "Co mogę dla pana zrobić" ('What can I do for you, sir.') (Marton et al. 1976:261). Pan ('sir'/Mr.') is hardly a generic word in Polish, but stretching the students' imagination to some extent one could, perhaps, convince them that pan should include pani ('ma'am'/Ms.'). But why, then, is the textbook not consistent in the omission of feminine forms instead of occasionally giving both the masculine and feminine forms in the Polish equivalents of the English words and phrases in the "Vocabulary study"? For example, the only child is translated as jedynak$_m$, jedynaczka$_f$, and the word conceited is explained with two feminine forms only: zarozumiała, próżna (although masculine forms are also possible). The reader of the textbook must realize that the use of the feminine forms (including females in the grammar) is determined by the contents of the dialogue preceding the "Vocabulary study", which mentions a girl who is an only child and who is conceited (1976:213). In other, male dominated contexts, English common gender nouns are translated into Polish masculine forms, e.g., "a colleague - kolega" (1976:159).

In Szkutnik (1979a) (a high school text) the exercise instructions, which are written in Polish, address students with the use of the masculine gender, e.g.,

Powiedz jakie miasta i kraje chciałbyś odwiedzić" (13).
('Say which cities and countries you would like to visit.')

Powiedz kim chciałbyś zostać (19).
('Say who you would like to become.')

One can also find a pseudo-generic use of the word człowiek ('man' - generic) in textbooks for teaching Polish. Człowiek can be used as a form of address, as in Człowieku, co robisz? ('Man, what are you doing?'). However, it is used almost exclusively to address males. Człowiek, therefore, has a very strong male bias as a mode of address. This is what learners of Polish discover when they read a dialogue between Paul and a train conductor (and its English translation) in Grala & Przywarska (1978:149-150). The conductor says to Paul: "Młody człowieku!" ('Young man!'), and it is translated into "Mister!". Nowhere in the book will the reader find Młody człowieku! translated into "Ma'am!"

Hartman & Judd (1978:389) say that "The use of Ms. as an alternative to denoting marital status is only beginning to reach textbooks." Although the authors do not explicitly propose the inclusion of this title in English textbooks, the reader of their article realizes that they would be in favour of such a change on a wider scale. Not all authors writing on sexism in FLM might be of the same opinion, however. Murdoch & Murdoch (1978:89) mention this title in the following context:

> Feminism, since the war at least, has taken a far less extravagant tone in England than in the USA. There has been no insistence in England that women be addressed by the conventional abbreviation for manuscript, and much of the entirely fruitless semantic hairsplitting has gone by the board.

Whether Ms. comes into use as a result of "fruitless semantic hairsplitting" or not, the fact remains that it is used by some native speakers, and this may be sufficient reason for its inclusion in FLM. No Polish textbook for English known to me ever mentions Ms. in any context.[8] This may seem more understandable, however, in light of the fact that some of the FLM exclude even the more traditional titles for females, i.e., Miss and Mrs. in contexts where their use would be expected:

> [...] w korespondencji mniej oficjalnej [...] wystepują na początku listu Dear Mr/Dr/Professor X [...] (Szkutnik & Pankhurst 1981a:179).
> ('In less formal correspondence, letters may begin with the following: Dear Mr/Dr/Professor X').

The last section of this chapter has been devoted to a discussion of sexist usage of language in some FLM. Some evidence has come from the target language of the textbooks, some from the native language of the learners. Apart from reasons stated earlier, sexism should be avoided to eliminate the possibility that female students will not be able to fully identify with the aim and contents of the textbooks, to reflect actual changes occurring in the target language, and to make the students and teachers aware of the consciousness-raising role of language[9].

Consider the following two examples of the use of English by Polish students (the first example comes from an oral presentation, the second from a written composition):

1. Teacher: What do pop stars spend their money on?
   Student: Pop stars spend their money on drugs, alcohol, cars, women ...
   Teacher: What about women pop stars?
   Student: Oh, women! They spend their money on clothes, cosmetics, lambswool pullovers [laughter].

2. They [people who drink] are rude to their wives, quarrel with them, beat their children, don't bring their salaries in, etc.

In both examples the students use English with a strong male bias. Of course, their native culture (Polish) may be fully responsible for this form of English usage, since they may have extended their native, male-dominated imagery/usage of Polish on the target language and culture. FLM cannot be blamed for being the sole instigators of sexism in students' use of the target language. However, there is no reason why FLM should serve to reinforce and justify sexist usage of the target language by foreign students.

Notes

1. Hartley (1978) is the only study devoted to the presentation of women in FLM known to me which states that the textbook examined is not sexist.
2. It is true that men are also shown to be late in Polish textbooks, but they seem to have "better" excuses.
3. The use of such impressionistic methodologies seems justified for these types of studies. This is confirmed by Rickel & Grant (1979:165) who did not find any differences and contradictions in the results of studies on the presentation of sex roles in the media and education, regardless of whether the methodologies used in these analyses were based on impressionistic or more sophisticated methodologies.
4. The respective texts are: the dialogue "I have too many defects" (Szkutnik & Pankhurst 1981a:277) and the monologue "Ann Green's reflections" (Szkutnik & Pankhurst 1981b:300-301).
5. Although in Polish the masculine gender also serves the function of the generic or common gender.
6. The dialogue is entitled "Jim's car", and Jim speaks about it with another male.
7. The following are just a few examples from Szkutnik and Pankhurst (1981a):

    Are you sure? Czy jesteś pewien? (183)
    Did you go to the pictures yesterday? Czy poszedłeś wczoraj do kina? (308)
    I couldn't work last Monday. Nie mogłem pracować w ubiegły poniedziałek. (321)
    I'll probably study English. Ja prawdopodobnie będę się uczył angielskiego. (333)
    Have you bought a car? Czy kupiłeś samochód? (346)

8. Ms. is not even mentioned in Falkowska et al. (1978a, 1978b), although they are fairly recent manuals for letter writing in English, and Ms. is predominantly used in writing.
9. See Judd (1983) for a related argument about the necessity for the inclusion of results of research on male/female language in foreign language teaching.

5

Sexism and stereotyping

This last chapter will review a few issues concerning language and sex. The problems discussed here cover a wide range of topics but I do not aim to present an in-depth analysis of any one of them. Instead, I will highlight several areas of language study which seem to merit further investigation, especially with regard to Polish. The selection of topics that follows below is biased in favour of those aspects of language use which place women in an inferior position. The inferior position of women is understood here to cover all those instances of sociolinguistic behaviour in which women, individually or as a group, are perceived and/or treated differently from the norm (=male), attributed certain traits and deprived of others on the basis of stereotyping, prejudice and false beliefs, confined to a limited range of activities, or denied the legal and moral right to self-determination. Apart from this, language use which associates positive values with male and masculine and negative values with female and feminine will also be regarded here as pertaining to the inferiority of women in society.

Are women and men talked about and referred to in the same way? The answer is - no, and it appears that the linguistic differences with regard to gender co-occur with linguistic and social inequality. In English, for example, there is a great contrast between sexually-paired words: masculine/male terms tend to evoke positive or neutral associations while feminine/female terms often acquire negative connotations. The classical examples of pairs of this type are <u>bachelor</u> : <u>spinster</u> and <u>master</u> : <u>mistress</u>. Strainchamps (1971) notes the sexist bias in sex-specific pairs of English words and states that when a word refers to either sex it is non-emotive, but when it refers exclusively to females, it is often derogatory. On the other hand, some words that were pejorative ceased to be so when they became exclusively masculine terms. The pair <u>shrewd</u> : <u>shrewish</u> is an example of both tendencies. In the sixteenth century they were sex-indefinite and meant 'wicked'. When they became sex-specific, their connotations diverged completely. Other denigrating terms for women, like virago, were once complimentary (virago used to mean 'heroic woman') and could also be used in reference to males. Schulz (1975) has compiled a list of about a thousand words and phrases which describe women in derogatory, sexual terms. There are not enough terms like this for men to even approach this figure. Schulz also observes that all of the pejorative terms for women were once neutral, and that the emotionally neutral terms of male reference do not undergo a symmetrical semantic derogation.

Kramer et al. (1978:643) report that "Researching terms for sexual promiscuity, Julia P. Stanley [1977] found 220 terms for a sexually promiscuous woman and only 22 for a promiscuous male. She notes that there is no linguistic reason why the first set is large and the latter small." Furthermore, if one uses a female term to refer to a man, an insult is usually intended. On the other hand, labelling a woman with a male term is not usually interpreted in the same way (Schulz 1975).

Similar research on the semantics of male vs. female designations is needed for Polish. Intuition suggests, however, that there are similar contrasts in Polish. For example, more terms seem to be used to refer to females than to males, and these are clearly associated with female sexuality and/or treatment of women as sex objects. Some of these include (these terms are not synonyms for 'prostitute' or 'nymphomaniac'):

decha (deska) - 'board';
dupa - 'ass';
dziura - 'hole';
lala (lalunia) - 'doll';
laska - 'stick';
mleczarnia - 'diary';
rura - 'pipe';
skóra - 'skin';
ujeżdżalnia - 'manège';
żyleta - 'razor blade'.

The variety of Polish words for men which would carry the same or similar sexual overtones is far more limited; none of the feminine terms listed above has its counterpart among the masculine terms.

There is also some indication (Jaworski 1985a) that in the area of sexual insults in Polish, the connotations of maleness and femaleness are not only different but also unequal. Some of the most obscene Polish insults directed at men identify them as female sexual organs ("inferior" to male organs), or as sexually passive and frigid (stereotypically female traits), or relegate them to the role of a female in a sexual act, which symbolically gives the speaker power over the insulted addressee. On the other hand, no insults sexually identifying women with men or male sexual organs are used, which indicates that treating a woman (at least linguistically) as a man is not insulting. Note also that the emotive connotations are different when a female is referred to with masculine or feminine gender forms.

Following are two hypothetically derived texts based on necrologies appearing in the Polish press:

1. Zmarła Janina Nowak. Odeszła od nas kobieta wielkiego charakteru i zasłużona pracowniczka Polskiego Radia.
2. Zmarła Janina Nowak. Odszedł od nas człowiek wielkiego charakteru i zasłużony pracownik Polskiego Radia.¹ ...

Choice of the masculine-gender referential is dictated by such facets as expression of respect or admiration, paying honor, or underlining outstanding characteristics of a person's personality. [...] A feeling of respect or esteem is generated by using the masculine gender referential while use of a feminine-gender lends a neutral meaning (Nalibov 1973:33-34).

Another dissimilarity between the terms of reference used with men and women in Polish appears in the use of titles (e.g., pan, pani) and names (FNs and LNs). In formal contexts (e.g., in the language of the press and in the language of live news bulletins) professional women, female politicians and other female public figures tend to be referred to with the form pani+(FN)LN. If the woman holds an occupational or professional title, this may be used in place of pani (or both may be used together), but even then it is more common to hear (and see) a phrase like Pani (Margaret) Thatcher ('Mrs. [Margaret] Thatcher') than Premier (Margaret) Thatcher ('Prime Minister [Margaret] Thatcher'). Polish speakers commonly agree that the use of pani in such contexts is an expression of politeness toward women. However, the use of pan as a title preceding a male's name would not, in the same context, be considered a politeness marker. Quite to the contrary, the use of Pan (Ronald) Reagan ('Mr. [Ronald] Reagan') instead of Prezydent (Ronald) Reagan ('President [Ronald] Reagan') is not polite but ironic and condescending. It becomes perfectly clear that politeness can be acutely asymmetrical (cf. Saporta 1979) and examples abound. For instance, in a recent issue of the leading women's weekly in Poland (Kobieta i Życie 4/1757, 23 January 1985, p. 10), a short article ("Amazonki" by 'Feliks') appeared, in which the author ridicules an anthology of papers on Western feminism published in Polish (Hołówka 1982). Feliks credits the afterword of the book to pani Aleksandra

Jasińska. He also refers to Simone de Beauvoir as pani Simone de Beauvoir and before that he says that "antologię opatrzono wstępem i posłowiem dwu uczonych pań-socjologów, bo odrzucam nawet myśl nazywania ich 'socjolożkami', co też jest męskim seksizmem."[2]

Pan Feliks probably thinks that referring to the two authors as dwie uczone panie-socjolog ('two learned lady sociologists') is not sexist, but most likely he would not have referred to them - if they were men - as dwaj uczeni panowie-socjologowie ('two learned gentlemen sociologists').

Radgowski's (1982) usage confirms the tentative hypothesis expressed in the last sentence. Discussing another book in Polish on foreign feminism (Sękalska 1980), Radgowski says: "Przypuszczam, że męscy feminiści powitają z entuzjazmem książkę pani Danuty Sękalskiej 'Kobieta wyzwolona?' [...] W błyskotliwym wstępie J.[erzy] Urban przestrzega nas przed traktowaniem Womens [sic] Liberation jako dziwactwa" [emphasis added] (Radgowski 1982:14).[3]

Women do not treat women any better. In her mass-oriented article ridiculing feminism Wisłocka (1984) reviews Hite (1976) quite unfavourably, especially in comparison with another book (Kinsey et al. 1953). What is more interesting, however, is the way Wisłocka refers to both authors: Kinsey, whom we also learn was a university professor, is referred to as Kinsey (5 times); Hite, whose Ph.D. received at Columbia is not mentioned, is referred to as pani Hite (8 times). Margaret Mead is treated in exactly the same way; Wisłocka refers to her as pani Margaret Mead. (Of course, there may be something "wrong" with Mead herself. Consider this: "In one ESL reader [...] Margaret Mead is repeatedly referred to as Miss Mead [not even Dr. Mead], while male authorities in the same book are frequently cited by last name only" [Hartman & Judd 1978:389].)

In Chapter 4, the stereotyping of women in foreign language materials has been documented. The stereotyping of women also takes place in other contexts in written and spoken Polish. It seems that the only two things that men cannot do in the area of childbirth and child-care is to give birth and breast-feed an infant. One of the things that (Polish) men do quite often when they become fathers is to give their babies a bath. But some Polish producers of bath thermometers do not want to accept the fathers' ability to do so and the instructions for their products remain addressed to "the young mother, the user of a bath thermometer."

On 7 September 1983, Polish Radio (Program I) presented a live report from an obstetric-gynecological hospital. In the introduction, one of the reporters said that the aim of the program was to bring the listener closer to the moment when new life begins, which was described as the happiest point in a woman's life. Evidence shows, however, that not every woman considers the moment of childbirth to be the happiest one in her life. Considering the data from countries other than Poland, it turns out "that in 1975 17 per cent of unmarried American female students who took part in one survey and 15 per cent of married Dutch women who took part in another, declared their intention not to have children" (Nicholson 1984:121).

Apart from social stereotyping, Polish speakers stereotype women's and men's speech. Whether or not this stereotyping accurately reflects the actual (if any) differences between the speech of Polish men and women is a question to which no answer can be given at this point. There seems to be a great need for future research to examine this issue with regard to Polish, and the work on male/female perceived/ actual speech differences in English provides a number of valuable insights about the methods which could be adopted for the study of Polish.

Kramer (1974, 1977) provides evidence which indicates that men's and women's speech is stereotyped differently in American English, and that there are also some differences in the way that males and females stereotype the linguistic behaviour of their own and the opposite sex (1977). In her 1977 study, Kramer's subjects associated the following traits as being more characteristic of males' speech: "demanding voice, deep voice, boastful, use swear words, dominating speech, loud speech, show anger rather than conceal it, straight to the point, militant speech, use slang, authoritarian speech, forceful speech, lounge and lean back while speaking, aggressive speech, sense of humor speech" (1977:158).

The speech of females was desribed as exhibiting more of the following traits: "enunciate clearly, high pitch, use hands and face to express ideas, gossip, concern for listener, gentle speech, fast speech, talk about trivial topics, wide range in rate and pitch, friendly speech, talk a lot, emotional speech, use many details, smooth speech, open and self-revealing speech, enthusiastic speech, smile a lot when talking, good grammar, polite speech, gibberish" (1977:158-159).

As Kramer (1977) notices, these stereotypes need not necessarily reflect the actual sex-based differences in the speech of American speakers, but seem to affect the real-life behaviour of men and women. With the media and education strengthening these stereotypes, and considering the competitive nature of American society, "it seems that male speech as described above is going to be considered more desirable economically" (Kramer 1977:159). Apart from some positive traits (open, self-revealing, gentle, polite, enthusiastic speech), female speech is, on the whole, perceived as ineffectual, containing more gossip and gibberish, and dealing with more trivial topics than male speech. (Kramer's findings on the sex-linked differences in assigning male and female speech certain stereotypical traits are not reported here.) In a final note, Kramer states that "The control females are perceived to have is not over the speech situation but over the grammatical forms they use. The control males are perceived to have is not over such things as word choice or pronunciation, but over the speech situation" (1977:159).

However, as Scott's (1980) research indicates the traits associated with stereotypical female speech are more positively valued, and are found to be more desirable for a competent adult speaker to adopt in communication than the traits associated with stereotypical male speech. Although this indicates, contrary to previous research (Lakoff 1975), that female speech need not be perceived as inferior, the speech of males remains more effective in real life, whereas females face the decision of whether they should stick to the socially preferred modes of communication, or abandon the prestige traits and adopt the effectiveness of male patterns.

In a study reviewing the research on sex-linked differences in speech, Berryman (1980) summarizes the "empirically validated generalizations of sex-based language which include:

1. Males more often assume a task or instrumental role and females a socio-emotional or expressive role when communicating.
2. Female speech is more likely than male speech to be characterized by correctness, especially in terms of pronunciation of the -ing suffix.
3. In mixed-sex dyadic interaction, males engage in more interruptions than females.
4. Males are likely to generate a greater volume of discourse than females.
5. The pitch of the female voice is higher than the pitch of the male voice.
6. Females' intonation patterns are characterized by more variability or expressiveness than males' intonation patterns" (Berryman 1980:200).

Using the above differences, Berryman had two speakers, one male and one female, use language in either of two ways: sex-appropriate and sex-inappropriate. Mixed-sex subjects then evaluated the sex-appropriate and sex-inappropriate linguistic behaviour of the male and the female speaker. Comparing the evaluations, Berryman was able to determine whether the perception of male/female speech is based only on identification of source gender, or also on the linguistic cues of male and female language. The results show that the evaluations of the male and female speakers were similar when they both used 'male' language (sex-appropriate for the man and sex-inappropriate for the woman), and that both speakers were evaluated similarly when they used 'female' language (sex-inappropriate for the man and sex-appropriate for the woman).

Berryman concludes that her study

> shows that male and female communicators are differently perceived. Additionally, a male speaker is rated differently depending on the specific language features he uses and a female speaker is rated differently depending on the specific features she uses. Language characteristics, and not source gender, were the main determinants of differential ratings in the study (Berryman 1980:207).

Kramarae (1982) points out, however, that there exists a large body of data (from experimental studies and from the analysis of folklinguistic statements about women's speech), which indicates that the negative stereotyping of female speech is still persistent in English, and that gender-differences in speech do occur. In the study of cultural attitudes toward the speech of females, Kramarae emphasizes the need for taking into account the folklinguistic opinions about the linguistic behaviour of women as reflected in proverbs, cartoons, etiquette guides and other records of culture. Although these are indirect sources of data they reflect some of the most salient attitudes toward the speech of women (and men).

As for advice books, Kramarae (1982) observes that most of the advice concerning speech is directed to women. Women are warned not to gossip, whereas men are advised not to make "derogatory remarks or questionable jokes about others" (Kramarae 1982:88).

American advice books also state that women should try to learn to discuss topics favoured by men, even though they will never be able to do this well. Women are advised to sound soft, agreeable, to keep their voices low, and to qualify their statements with expressions like "I think this is so". The suggestion that women's statements be qualified (a female speech characteristic, which according to college students' opinions makes women sound stupid [Kramer 1974]) reflects the more general tendency to regard women's minds as more intuitive rather than analytical and the belief that a woman has a "man's" mind when she proves to be logical.

Kramarae also quotes an excerpt from Post's etiquette books which places women's thinking and verbal behaviour in a modest and reticent position:

> The perfect secretary should forget that she is a human being, and be the most completely efficient aid at all times and on all subjects. ... She should respond to [her boss's] requirements exactly as a machine responds to the touch of lever [sic] or accelerator. If he says 'Good

morning,' she answers 'Good morning' with a smile and cheerfully. She does not volunteer a remark - unless she has messages of importance to give him. If he says nothing, she says nothing, and she does not even mentally notice that he had said nothing (1945, 548) (Kramarae 1982:88).

The above quote indicates the sub-human categorization of women. This interesting asymmetry between a secretary and her boss results not only from a perception of the social and professional inequality between them, but also from the fact that the submissiveness of a secretary to her boss is that of a woman to a man. The importance of the sex factor, rather than social and professional dependance in unequal relations at work, is also present in the attitudes expressed toward women holding managerial positions in Poland. In a book for managerial women (Kozłowska & Strzelecka 1970), the problem of male bosses propositioning their female colleagues (not vice versa!) is discussed, and the unquestioned consequences of such relations for women seem to be more severe than for men.

> Adoracja szefa wyższej rangi nie pomaga kobiecie w zawodowej karierze. Otoczenie bowiem częściej tłumaczy jej zawodowe sukcesy poparciem szefa niż jej własnymi zdolnościami i pracą, co jest dla niej przykre.
> Ponadto grozi to zawsze komplikacjami w jej własnym życiu rodzinnym. Rozwód mężczyzny szefa wyższej rangi w celu małżeństwa z kobietą szefem jest zwykle takim skandalem obyczajowym w środowisku, że powoduje odejście kobiety ze środowiska kierowniczego.
> Dlatego kobieta szef nie powinna być zainteresowana w podtrzymywaniu adoracji szefa wyższej rangi [emphasis added] (Kozłowska & Strzelecka 1970).

What is surprising here is the fact that women are the sole addressees of this passage; men are not told that they should not make women's careers more difficult, and it is not even suggested that men leave their positions in the wake of a scandalous affair.

Women are even made to feel responsible for the insulting behaviour of their male colleagues. Nothing about how men should (or should not) behave is stated in the following passage, and no mention is made of how women could improve their own status:

> Bywa, że szef wyższej rangi zachowuje się prymitywnie i wulgarnie. Należy jednak podkreślić, że zwykle postępuje tak dopiero po nieopatrznej zachęcie ze strony kobiety. Wówczas najlepiej zmienić miejsce pracy, przenieść się do innej jednostki, zachowując maksimum dyskrecji co do przyczyn takiej decyzji oraz maksimum taktu w stosunku do szefa, który

jest tego przyczyną [emphasis added] (Kozłowska & Strzelecka 1970: 76).[5]

The books of two Polish authorities on etiquette (Kamyczek 1956; Gumowska 1969) are also good examples of how male and female verbal behaviour is stereotyped. Kamyczek's chapter on public speaking, "Głos ma kolega Nowak ..." ('Colleague Nowak has the floor ...') presents exclusively male imagery, so that the reader has no doubt that public speaking is a male domain. Male imagery is further maintained by the use of the false generic człowiek (e.g., "młody człowiek może w przyszłosci stać się niezłym mówcą" [1956:153] ['A young man may, in the future, become a good speaker.']), and by the indication that the hypothetical speaker is a male (i.e., he is advised before giving a speech to say to himself several times: "Nie będę się bał mówić. Będę przemawiał odważnie" [1956:55] ['I am not going to be afraid of speaking. I am going to speak with confidence.']).

When Kamyczek gives advice on how to initiate a conversation at a dance, the advice is for men. Accordingly, bad or 'risky' jokes should be avoided, especially in the company of women. Shy men are advised to let women do the talking.

The asymmetrical treatment of men and women is also apparent in sections dealing with social introductions. First Kamyczek says that when "you" (=male reader [?]) are introduced to someone else without mentioning "your" name, then "you" are obliged to say it "yourself". Kamyczek then adds that women should also give their names. That a woman should not do so is considered by the author an outdated custom.

Gumowska (1969) also treats men and women separately when she discusses the exchange of names, and demonstrates a puzzling inconsistency, which results in further restricting women's speech. First, Gumowska says: "Pan przedstawiając się pani ma obowiązek wymienić swoje nazwisko, ona nie musi, ale może" (1969:67-68).[6] A moment later, however, the same author adds: "Reguła nakazuje, by w kontaktach towarzyskich kobieta raczej nie przedstawiała się mężczyźnie. Powinna natomiast robić to w związku ze swoją działalnością zawodową" (1969:68).[7]

Women's speech is also considered different from men's when supposed female irrationality is contrasted with males' straightforward use of language:

> Dwa są sposoby na to, by dowiedzieć się, czy ktoś nas kocha [...] Jeden sposób, głównie przez niewiasty używany, to obskubywanie płatków stokrotki. Mężczyźni uciekają się do drugiego sposobu, to znaczy stawiają danej osobie odpowiednio sformułowane pytanie (Kamyczek 1956:166).[8]

Most of the time, both etiquette books address their readers as if they were all men. When they have something to say to women, they (women) are not addressed directly but are spoken of in the third person. Such is also the case when Kamyczek gives advice on how to behave in order to please one's host at a party. Here Kamyczek says that "Gość niewiasta sprawi dodatkową radość gospodyni, pytając o przepis na kruche ciastka" (1956:118).[9] Of course, when the topic of the conversation concerns housekeeping and cooking, the speakers are all female. Likewise, stupid, excessive, hysterical talk, as well as giggling and other negative stereotypes, are associated exclusively with women (for more examples see Jaworski 1985:173-174).

Humour provides more examples of the sexist stereotyping of speech. A detailed survey of cartoon captions and other forms of verbal humour in Polish is necessary to find all the patterns of sexism in this field, but it is not difficult to pinpoint sexism even in casually encountered jokes appearing in print in Poland. Among the dozens of sexist jokes printed on the last page of an extremely popular Polish weekly (Przekrój) there are many which deal with female talkativeness, gossiping, nagging, etc. For example:

- Mózg Falczakowej można często zobaczyć na końcu jej języka (Przekrój 2049, 16 September 1984).[10]

- Nie macie pojęcia - skarży się Falczak - jak Falczakowa lubi gadać, gadać, gadać, gadać, gadać, gadać, gadać, gadać i gadać (Przekrój 2059, 25 November 1984).[11]

In order to understand better the male-female relations in society, it seems crucial to discover the actual and perceived differences in the speech of men and women, and to make sure which of the differences (if any) are real and which are myths created and reinforced by stereotypes (see Smith 1985 for an excellent treatment of this and related topics). While relying on folklinguistic assumptions in accounting for male-female language may be misleading and merely perpetuate false beliefs about males and females (Coates 1984), the study of these folklinguistic assumptions and attitudes should also prove to be of great value in language and sex research.

Notes

1. Janina Nowak has died. A woman of great character and a worthy employee of the Polish Radio has left us.
   Janina Nowak has died. A man [generic] of great character and a worthy employee of the Polish Radio has left us.
2. [...] the anthology was provided with an introduction and an afterword by two learned lady sociologists, because I even reject the idea of calling them "sociologistesses", which also constitutes male sexism.
3. I suppose that male feminists will greet Ms. Danuta Sękalska's book, "Kobieta wyzwolona?" ['The liberated woman?'] with enthusiasm. In his brilliant introduction J.[erzy] Urban warns us against treating Women's Liberation as an eccentricity [emphasis added].
4. A higher-rank boss's adoration for a woman does not help her in her work. If this were the case, her colleagues would more readily account for her professional success with the support she gets from her boss rather than with her own abilities and work, which would upset her.
   Moreover, this would always cause complications in her own family life. The divorce of a male boss of higher rank in order to marry a female boss is usually regarded as such a scandalous affair by their associates that it causes the woman to leave the managerial circle.
   Therefore, a female boss should not be interested in maintaining the adoration of a higher-rank boss [emphasis added].
5. It happens that a higher-rank boss behaves in a primitive and vulgar way. One should emphasize, however, that he usually does so after a woman recklessly encourages him to do so. In such a case, it is best to change jobs and move to another unit while maintaining a maximum of discretion as to the reason for this decision and a maximum of tact with the boss who is its cause [emphasis added].
6. A gentleman introducing himself to a lady is obliged to give his name; she needn't but may do so.
7. In social relations the rule prescribes that a woman should not introduce herself to a man. She should do this, however, in connection with her professional activities.
8. There are two ways to find out if someone loves us. One way, mainly used by women, is to pluck the petals from a daisy. Men resort to the other way, that is, asking a given person an appropriately formulated question.
9. A female guest will give additional pleasure to the hostess when she asks for the recipe for the cookies.
10. - Falczakowa's brain can often be seen on the tip of her tongue.
11. - You have no idea - complains Falczak - how Falczakowa likes to talk, talk, talk, talk, talk, talk, talk, and talk.

Conclusion

This book has pointed out some of the ways in which language can be used to express speakers' sexist attitudes. The manifestations of these attitudes are numerous: they are either overt, as in blatant statements of women's inferiority to men, or covert, as in the use of masculine generics which render women linguistically invisible. Similar concepts acquire different connotations depending on whether they are associated with males or females. It has become quite appropriate to joke about women as a group, but not about men. Stupid talk and unimportant talk are associated more readily with women than with men. No matter what the form of sexism, most of it takes place through the use of language and, thus, is appropriately labelled **linguistic sexism**.

Whereas in English a considerable body of data on sexism and sex-related differences in language is already available, the study of these topics in Polish is still at the preliminary stage of formulating hypotheses and methodology. Undoubtedly, the existing research on English should serve as one of the major bases for developing a sound sociolinguistic investigation of the relation between language and sex in Polish.

Naturally, the problems related to the study of language and sex discussed in this short book do not represent an exhaustive listing. Further investigations of sex-linked differences in the use and perception of language with regard to Polish may include, among others, the following topics (which have already received some attention in English): ways in which language is used by mothers and fathers with their children (Engle 1980; Greif 1980; for some German data see Pieper 1984); women's and men's use and reactions to obscenity (Rieber, Wiedemann & D'Amato 1979); the organization of females' and males' verbal culture (Jones 1980; Bruner & Kelso 1980); non-verbal behaviour between males and females (Henley 1977); patterns of interruptions and turn-taking in mixed-sex dyads (Zimmerman & West 1975;

Kennedy & Camden 1981), and many others.

It has also been suggested that students' misuse of sex-specific forms in a foreign language may be a possible area of study for a sociolinguist interested in the problem of cross-cultural communication (Janicki 1980; for a survey of cross-linguistic differences in linguistic behaviour between men and women see Bodine 1975a; Saville-Troike 1982).

If this book at least managed to demonstrate the need for a continued study of language in relation to sex - and linguistic sexism in particular - then one of its primary goals has been realized.

Appendix

The following are complete versions of the exercises used in the experiments discussed in Chapters 1 and 2.

Experiment 1 (Chapter 1).

Exercise I

Ułóz 5 zdań z podanymi poniżej przymiotnikami.
1. ambitny
2. dokładny
3. obowiązkowy
4. pracowity
5. dzielny

Exercise II

Ułóz 5 zdań z podanymi poniżej przymiotnikami.
1. ambitna
2. dokładna
3. obowiązkowa
4. pracowita
5. dzielna

Exercise III

Ułóz 5 zdań z podanymi poniżej przymiotnikami.
1. ambitny/ambitna
2. dokładny/dokładna
3. obowiązkowy/obowiązkowa

4. pracowity/pracowita
5. dzielny/dzielna   (Based on Gawdzik 1980:55)

Experiment 2 (Chapter 1).

Exercise I
Ułóz 6 zdań. W każdym z nich zastosuj wybrane określenie cechy charakteru.
1. rozważny - najpierw pomyśli zanim coś zrobi
2. skromny - nie podkreśla swoich zasług
3. uczciwy - nie przywłaszcza sobie cudzej rzeczy ani wyników cudzej pracy, nie działa na cudzą szkodę
4. uczynny - pomaga innym, chociaż nie musi
5. uspołeczniony - podejmuje się pracy na rzecz ogółu, nie licząc na osobistą korzyść, czynnie występuje w obronie ładu społecznego lub społecznej własności
6. wrażliwy - martwi się kłopotami i cierpieniami innych ludzi

Exercise II
Ułóz 6 zdań. W każdym z nich zastosuj wybrane określenie cechy charakteru.
1. rozważna - najpierw pomyśli zanim coś zrobi
2. skromna - nie podkreśla swoich zasług
3. uczciwa - nie przywłaszcza sobie cudzej rzeczy ani wyników cudzej pracy, nie działa na cudzą szkodę
4. uczynna - pomaga innym, chociaż nie musi
5. uspołeczniona - podejmuje się pracy na rzecz ogólu, nie licząc na osobistą korzyść, czynnie występuje w obronie ładu społecznego lub społecznej własności
6. wrażliwa - martwi się kłopotami i cierpieniami innych ludzi

Exercise III
Ułóz 6 zdań. W każdym z nich zastosuj wybrane określenie cechy charakteru.
1. rozważny/rozważna - najpierw pomyśli zanim coś zrobi
2. skromny/skromna - nie podkreśla swoich zasług
3. uczciwy/uczciwa - nie przywłaszcza sobie cudzej rzeczy ani wyników cudzej pracy, nie działa na cudzą szkodę
4. uczynny/uczynna - pomaga innym chociaż nie musi

5. uspołeczniony/uspołeczniona - podejmuje się pracy na rzecz ogółu, nie licząc na osobistą korzyść, czynnie występuje w obronie ładu społecznego lub społecznej własności
6. wrażliwy/wrażliwa - martwi się kłopotami i cierpieniami innych ludzi

(Based on Gawdzik 1980:155)

Experiment 3 (Chapter 2)

Exercise I

Podaj nazwy zawodów:
1. Człowiek, który leczy chorych to ....
2. Człowiek, który uczy w szkole to ....
3. Człowiek, który pisze wiersze to ....
4. Człowiek, który zapowiada program TV to ....
5. Człowiek, który czesze innym włosy to ....
6. Człowiek, który mierzy temperaturę i robi zastrzyki chorym w szpitalu to ....
7. Człowiek, który kieruje ruchem ulicznym to ....
8. Człowiek, który sprzedaje w sklepie to ....
9. Człowiek, który uczy się na uniwersytecie to ....
10. Człowiek, który roznosi listy to ....
11. Człowiek, który sprząta biura i szkoły to ....
12. Człowiek, który podaje posiłki w restauracji to ....
13. Człowiek, który zajmuje się dziećmi w przedszkolu to ....
14. Człowiek, który pierze innym bieliznę to ....
15. Człowiek, który gotuje posiłki w restauracji to ....

Exercise II

Podaj nazwy zawodów:
1. Osoba, która leczy chorych to ....
2. Osoba, która uczy w szkole to ....
3. Osoba, która pisze wiersze to ....
4. Osoba, która zapowiada program TV to ....
5. Osoba, która czesze innym włosy to ....

6. Osoba, która mierzy temperaturę i robi zastrzyki chorym w szpitalu to ....
7. Osoba, która kieruje ruchem ulicznym to ....
8. Osoba, która sprzedaje w sklepie to ....
9. Osoba, która uczy się na uniwersytecie to ....
10. Osoba, która roznosi listy to ....
11. Osoba, która sprząta biura i szkoły to ....
12. Osoba, która podaje posiłki w restauracji to ....
13. Osoba, która zajmuje się dziećmi w przedszkolu to ....
14. Osoba, która pierze innym bieliznę to ....
15. Osoba, która podaje posiłki w restauracji to ....

Exercise III
Podaj nazwy zawodów:
1. leczy chorych - ....
2. uczy w szkole - ....
3. pisze wiersze - ....
4. zapowiada program TV - ....
5. czesze innym włosy - ....
6. mierzy temperaturę i robi zastrzyki chorym w szpitalu - ....
7. kieruje ruchem ulicznym - ....
8. sprzedaje w sklepie - ....
9. uczy się na uniwersytecie - ....
10. roznosi listy - ....
11. sprząta biura i szkoły - ....
12. podaje posiłki w restauracji - ....
13. zajmuje się dziećmi w przedszkolu - ....
14. pierze innym bieliznę - ....
15. gotuje posiłki w restauracji - ....

References

Abbot, G. 1984. "Unisex 'they'". ELT Journal 38/1. 45-48.
Albee, G.W. 1981. "The prevention of sexism". Professional Psychology 12/1. 20-28.
American Psychological Association. 1977. Guidelines for nonsexist language in APA journals. (Publication Manual Change Sheet 2). Washington D.C.: American Psychological Association.
Andrzejewski, J. 1982. Miazga. Warszawa: Państwowy Instytut Wydawniczy.
BSIG = Basic skills in grammar 2. 1976 rev. ed. Cambridge: The Adult Education Company.
Basso, K.H. & H.A. Selby (eds). 1976. Meaning in anthropology. Albuquerque: University of New Mexico Press.
Bate, B. 1975. "Generic man, invisible woman: Language, thought and social change". University of Michigan Papers in Women's Studies 2 (1). 83-95.
Bąk, P. 1978. Gramatyka języka polskiego. Warszawa: Wiedza Powszechna.
Bendix, E.H. 1977. "Linguistic models as political symbols: Gender and the generic 'he' in English". In Orasanu, J., M.K. Slater & L.L. Adler (eds). 1977. 23-39.
Berryman, C.L. 1980. "Attitudes toward male and female language". In Berryman, C.L. & V.A. Eman (eds). 1980. 195-216.
Berryman, C.L. & V.A. Eman (eds). 1980. Communication, language and sex: Proceedings of the First Annual Conference. Rowley, Mass.: Newbury House.
Bidwell, J.S. 1978. "Sexism in the foreign-language classroom". In Freudenstein, R. (ed.). 1978. 41-47.
Biliński, W. 1983. Wyjaśnienie. Warszawa: Książka i Wiedza.
Blaubergs, M. 1980. "An analysis of classic arguments against changing sexist language". Women's Studies International Quarterly 3. 135-147.
Bodine, A. 1975. "Androcentrism in prescriptive grammar: Singular 'they', sex-indefinite 'he', and 'he or she'". Language in Society 4. 129-146.

Bodine, A. 1975a. "Sex differentiation in language". In Thorne, B. & N. Henley (eds). 1975. 130-151.
Bodine, A. 1977. "Review of Key (1975)". Language in Society 6. 104-110.
Bohdziewicz, P. 1981. Absolwent. Warszawa: Iskry.
Bressan, D. 1978. "Italiano Vivo' and its women". In Freudenstein, R. (ed.). 1978. 25-31.
Brogynayi, B. (ed.). 1979. Festschrift für Oswald Szemerenyi on the occasion of his sixty-fifth birthday. Amsterdam: John Benjamins.
Brouwer, D., M. Gerritsen & D. de Haan 1979. "Speech differences between women and men: On the wrong track?" Language in Society 8. 33-50.
Brower, R.A. (ed.). 1959. On translation. Cambridge: Harvard University Press.
Brown, R. & M. Ford 1961. "Address in American English". Journal of Abnormal and Social Psychology 62/2. 375-385.
Brown, R. & A. Gilman 1972. "Pronouns of power and solidarity". In Giglioli, P.P. (ed.). 1972. 252-282.
Bruner, E.M. & J.P. Kelso 1980. "Gender differences in grafitti: A semiotic perspective". Women's Studies International Quarterly 3. 239-252.
Brückner, A. 1916. "Ty-wy-pan: Kartka z dziejów próżności ludzkiej". Kraków: L.K. Górski.
Brzechwa, J. 1963. Sto bajek. Warszawa: Czytelnik.
Burr, E., S. Dunn & N. Farquhar 1972. "The language of inequality". ETC.: A Review of General Semantics 29. 414-416.
Butturff, D. & E.L. Epstein (eds). 1978. Women's language and style. Published with the assistance of the Dept. of English, University of Akron.
Cameron, D. 1985. "What has gender got to do with sex?" Language & Communication 5/1. 19-27.
Carroll, F.W. 1978. "The limits of my language are the limits of my world". In Freudenstein, R. (ed.). 1978. 49-60.
Casagrande, J. (ed.). 1983. The linguistic connection. Lanham, MD.: University Press of America.
Ciapało, M. 1983. Incydent. Łódź: Wydawnictwo Łódzkie.
Clark, H. & E. Clark. 1977. Psychology and language: An introduction to psycholinguistics. New York: Harcourt Brace and Jovanovich, Inc.
Clarricoates, K. 1978. "'Dinosaurs are in the classroom' - a re-examination of some aspects of hidden curriculum in primary schools". Women's Studies International Quarterly 1. 353-364.

Coates, J. 1984. "Language and sexism". CLIE Working Paper No. 5. BAAL/LAGB Committee for Linguistics in Education.

Cooper, R.L. 1984. "The avoidance of androcentric generics". International Journal of the Sociology of Language 50. 5-20.

Corbett, G.G. 1983. "The number of genders in Polish". Papers and Studies in Contrastive Linguistics 16. 83-89.

Coulmas, F. (ed.). 1979. Conversational routine. The Hague: Mouton.

Crosby, F. & L. Nyquist 1977. "The female register: An empirical study of Lakoff's hypotheses". Language in Society 6. 313-322.

Dahlberg, F. (ed.). 1981. Woman the gatherer. New Haven: Yale University Press.

Dobkin de Rios, M. 1978. "Why women don't hunt: An anthropologist looks at the origin of the sexual division of labor in society". Women's Studies 5. 241-247.

Doroszewski, W. (ed.). 1958-1969. Słownik języka polskiego. Warszawa.

Dubois, B.L. & I. Crouch 1975. "The question of tag questions in women's speech: They don't really use more of them, do they?" Language in Society 4. 284-294.

Engle, M. 1980. "Family influences on the language development of young children". Women's Studies International Quarterly 3. 259-266.

Ervin-Tripp, S.M. 1973a. "The connotations of gender". In Ervin-Tripp, S.M. 1973b. 156-172.

Ervin-Tripp, S.M. 1973b. Language acquisition and communicative choice: Essays by Susan M. Ervin-Tripp. Selected and introduced by Anwar S. Dil. Stanford: Stanford University Press.

Ervin-Tripp, S.M. 1976. "Speech acts and social learning". In Basso, K.H. & H.A. Selby (eds). 1976. 123-153.

Falkowska, M. et al. 1978a. Wzory listów angielskich. Wrocław: Wiedza Powszechna.

Falkowska, M. et al. 1978b. Korespondencja w języku angielskim. Wrocław: Ossolineum.

Fillmore, C.J. 1984. "Remarks on contrastive pragmatics". In Fisiak, J. (ed.). 1984. 119-141.

Fisiak, J. 1963. "Kategorie rodzaju rzeczowników zapożyczonych z języka angielskiego". Rozprawy Komisji Językoznawczej ŁTN 9. 63-68.

Fisiak, J. 1975. "Some remarks concerning the noun gender assignment of loanwords". Biuletyn Polskiego Towarzystwa Językoznawczego 33. 59-63.

Fisiak, J. (ed.). 1981. Contrastive linguistics and the language teacher. Oxford: Pergamon Press.

Fisiak, J. (ed.). 1984. Contrastive linguistics: Prospects and problems. Berlin: Mouton.

Fisiak, J., M. Lipińska-Grzegorek & T. Zabrocki 1978. An introductory English-Polish contrastive grammar. Warszawa: Państwowe Wydawnictwo Naukowe.

Freudenstein, R. (ed.). 1978. The role of women in foreign-language textbooks: A collection of essays. Brussels: AIMAV & Didier.

Gaff, R. 1982. "Sex-stereotyping in modern language teaching - an aspect of the hidden curriculum". The British Journal of Language Teaching 2/2. 71-78.

Gawdzik, W. 1980. Nasza mowa - nasz świat: Klasa 3. Warszawa: Wydawnictwa Szkolne i Pedagogiczne.

Giglioli, P.P. (ed.). 1972. Language and social context. Harmondsworth: Penguin.

The golden picture dictionary for beginning readers. 1972. Racine, Wis.: Western Publishing Company.

Gornick, V. & B.K. Moran (eds). 1971. Woman in sexist society: Studies in power and powerlessness. New York: Basic Books.

Grala, M. & W. Przywarska 1978. Z polskim na co dzień: An intermediate course for English speakers. Warszawa: Państwowe Wydawnictwo Naukowe.

Grandcolas, B. 1978. "The role of women in 'Speak English'". In Freudenstein, R. (ed.). 1978. 65-72.

Gregersen, E.A. 1979. "Sexual linguistics". In Orasanu, J., M.K. Slater & L.L. Adler (eds). 1979. 3-19.

Greif, E.B. 1980. "Sex differences in parent-child conversations". Women's Studies International Quarterly 3. 253-258.

Grzegorczykowa, R., R. Laskowski & H. Wróbel (eds). 1984. Gramatyka współczesnego języka polskiego - morfologia. Warszawa: Państwowe Wydawnictwo Naukowe.

Gumowska, I. 1969. ABC dobrego wychowania. Warszawa: Wiedza Powszechna.

Hardman-de-Bautista, M.J. 1978. "Linguistic postulate and applied anthropological linguistics". In Honsa, V. & M.J. Hardman-de-Bautista (eds). 1978. 117-136.

Hartley, G.C. 1978. "The role of women in 'Le Français et la Vie'". In Freudenstein, R. (ed.). 1978. 73-83.

Hartman, P.L. & E.L. Judd 1978. "Sexism and TESOL materials". TESOL Quarterly 12/4. 383-393.

Hellinger, M. 1980. "'For men must work, and women must weep': Sexism in English language textbooks used in German schools". Women's Studies International Quarterly 3. 267-275.

Henley, N.M. 1977. Body politics: Power, sex, and non-verbal communication. Englewood Cliffs, N.J.: Prentice-Hall.

Henley, N. & B. Thorne 1975. "Sex differences in language, speech, and nonverbal communication: An annotated bibliography". In Thorne, B. & N. Henley (eds). 1975. 204-305.
Herbert, R.K. & B. Nykiel-Herbert forthcoming. "Explorations in linguistic sexism: A contrastive sketch". Papers and Studies in Contrastive Linguistics 21.
Hill, P. 1980. "Women in the world of ELT textbooks 1979/80". E.F.L. Gazette Part I June, 4-5; Part II July, 2.
Hite, S. 1976. The Hite report: A nationwide study on female sexuality. New York: Macmillan.
Hołówka, T. (ed.). 1982. Nikt nie rodzi się kobietą. Warszawa: Czytelnik.
Honsa, V. & M.J. Hardman-de-Bautista (eds). 1978. Papers on linguistics and child language. The Hague: Mouton.
Hook, D.D. 1974. "Sexism in English pronouns and forms of address". General Linguistics 14/2. 86-96.
Huddleston, R. 1984. Introduction to the grammar of English. Cambridge: Cambridge University Press.
Hudson, R.A. 1980. Sociolinguistics. Cambridge: Cambridge University Press.
Ibrahim, M.H. 1973. Grammatical gender: Its origin and development. The Hague: Mouton.
Ittzés, K. 1978. "Hungarian women in reality". In Freudenstein, R. (ed.). 1978. 9-24.
Jakobson, R. 1959. "On linguistic aspects of translation". In Brower, R.A. (ed.). 1959. 232-239.
Janicki, K. 1979. "Contrastive sociolinguistics - some considerations". Papers and Studies in Contrastive Linguistics 10. 33-40.
Janicki, K. 1980. "Deviance beyond grammar". Studia Anglica Posnaniensia 12. 61-71.
Janicki, K. 1984. "Contrastive linguistics reconsidered". Papers and Studies in Contrastive Linguistics 18. 15-29.
Jaworski, A. 1982. "Formy zwracania się do drugich w wojsku: Analiza socjolingwistyczna". Język Polski 62. 266-270.
Jaworski, A. 1983. "Sexism in textbooks". The British Journal of Language Teaching 21/2. 109-113.
Jaworski, A. 1985. "A linguistic picture of women's position in society". Unpublished Ph.D. dissertation. Adam Mickiewicz University, Poznań.
Jaworski, A. 1985a. "A note on sexism and insulting with examples from Polish". Maledicta: The International Journal of Verbal Aggression 9.
Johnson, B.D. 1983. "Female terror at the terminal". Maclean's: Canada's Weekly

Magazine 96/29. 45-46.

Johnson, J. 1984. "Variations in Polish nasal /e/: A contribution to the development of contrastive sociolinguistic methodology". Papers and Studies in Contrastive Linguistics 18. 31-41.

Jones, D. 1980. "Gossip: Notes on women's oral culture". Women's Studies International Quarterly 3. 193-198.

Judd, E. 1983. "The problem of applying sociolinguistic findings to TESOL: The case of male/female language". In Wolson, N. & E. Judd (eds). 1983. 234-241.

Kamyczek, J. 1956. Grzeczność na co dzień. Warszawa: Iskry.

Kamyczek, J. 1974[6]. Grzeczność na co dzień. Warszawa: Iskry.

Kennedy, C.W. & C.T. Camden 1981. "Gender differences in interruption behavior: A dominance perspective". International Journal of Women's Studies 4/2. 135-142.

Key, M.R. 1972. "Linguistic behavior of male and female". Linguistics 88. 15-31.

Key, M.R. 1975. Male/female language. Methuen: The Scarecrow Press.

Kinsey, A.C. et al. 1953. Sexual behavior in human female. Philadelphia.

Klemensiewicz, Z. 1946. "Pan i obywatel". Język Polski 26. 33-42.

Klemensiewicz, Z. 1981[10]. Podstawowe wiadomości z gramatyki języka polskiego. Warszawa: Państwowe Wydawnictwo Naukowe.

Klemensiewicz, Z. 1982a [1957]. "Tytuły i nazwy zawodowe kobiet". In Klemensiewicz, Z. 1982b. 729-753.

Klemensiewicz, Z. 1982b. Składnia, stylistyka, pedagogika językowa: Wybór prac pod redakcją Anny Kałkowskiej. Warszawa: Państwowe Wydawnictwo Naukowe.

Kozakiewicz, M. 1962. O miłości prawie wszystko. Warszawa: Ludowa Spółdzielnia Wydawnicza.

Kozłowska, H. & I. Strzelecka 1970. Problemy kobiet szefów. Warszawa: Zakład Wydawnictw CRS.

Kramarae, C. 1981. Men and women speaking. Rowley, Mass.: Newbury House.

Kramarae, C. 1982. "Gender: How she speaks". In Ryan, E.B. & H. Giles (eds). 1982. 84-98.

Kramer, C. 1974. "Stereotypes of women's speech: The word of cartoons". Journal of Popular Culture 8. 624-630.

Kramer, C. 1975. "Sex-related differences in address systems". Anthropological Linguistics 15/5. 198-210.

Kramer, C. 1977. "Perceptions of female and male speech". Language and Speech 20. 151-161.

Kramer, C., B. Thorne & N. Henley 1978. "Perspectives on language and communication". Signs: Journal of Women in Culture and Society 3/3. 638-651.

Kürschner, W. & R. Vogt (eds). 1985. Sprachtheorie, Pragmatik, Interdisziplinäres: Akten des 19. Linguistischen Kolloquiums, Vechta 1984. Band 2. Tübingen: Niemeyer.

Lakoff, R. 1975. Language and woman's place. New York: Harper and Row.

Lyons, J. Semantics. Vol. 2. Cambridge: Cambridge University Press.

Łoś, J. 1916. "Od 'ty' do 'pan'". Język Polski 3. 1-10.

MacKay, D.G. 1980. "On the goals, principles, and procedures for prescriptive grammar: Singular they". Language in Society 9. 349-367.

MacKay, D.G. & D.C. Fulkerson 1979. "On the comprehension and production of pronouns". Journal of Verbal Learning and Verbal Behavior 18. 661-673.

MacKay, D.G. & T. Konishi 1980. "Personification and the pronoun problem". Women's Studies International Quarterly 3. 149-163.

Manes, J. 1981. "Review of Mathiot (1979c)". Language in Society 10. 261-269.

Marton, W., E. Lebelt & L. Grochowska 1976. English in structures and situations. Warszawa: Państwowe Wydawnictwo Naukowe.

Martyna, W. 1980a. "Teaching about language and the sexes". Women's Studies International Quarterly 3. 295-303.

Martyna, W. 1980b. "Beyond the 'He/Man' approach: The case for nonsexist language". Signs: Journal of Women in Culture and Society 5/3. 482-493.

Martyna, W. 1980c. "The psychology of the generic masculine". In McConnell-Ginet, S., R. Borker & N. Furman (eds). 1980. 69-78.

Martyniak, Z. 1976. "Wstęp". In Townsend, R. 1976. 5-8.

Mathiot, M. 1979a. (assisted by M. Roberts). "Sex roles as revealed through referential gender in American English". In Mathiot, M. (ed.). 1979c. 1-47.

Mathiot, M. 1979b. "Folk definitions as a tool for the analysis of lexical meaning". In Mathiot, M. (ed.). 1979c. 121-260.

Mathiot, M. (ed.). 1979c. Ethnolinguistics: Boas, Sapir and Whorf revisited. The Hague: Mouton.

McConnell-Ginet, S. 1978. "Address forms in sexual politics". In Butturff, D. & E.L. Epstein (eds). 1978. 23-35.

McConnell-Ginet, S. 1979. "Prototypes, pronouns and person". In Mathiot, M. (ed.). 1979c. 63-83.

McConnell-Ginet, S. 1980. "Linguistics and the feminist challenge". In McConnell-Ginet, S., R. Borker & N. Furman (eds). 1980. 3-25.

McConnell-Ginet, S., R. Borker & N. Furman (eds). 1980. Women and language in literature and society. New York: Praeger.

Michalska, M. & C. Beven-Oyrzanowska 1977[4]. I learn English. Warszawa: Wiedza Powszechna.

Mikulska, A. 1980[3]. Play and learn. Book 1 & 2, Book 3 & 4. Warszawa: Wiedza Powszechna.

Miller, C. & K. Swift 1972. "One small step for genkind". New York Times Magazine. April 16, 1972. 364.

Miller, C. & K. Swift 1976. Words and women: New language in new times. Garden City, N.Y.: Anchor Press/Doubleday.

Miller, C. & K. Swift. 1981. The handbook of non-sexist writing for writers, editors and speakers: British edition revised by Stephanie Dowrich. London: The Women's Press.

Miller, D.G. 1977. "Tripartization, sexism and the rise of the feminine gender in Indo-European". The Florida Journal of Anthropology 2. 3-16.

Miller, D.G. 1983. "English vs. woman". In Casagrande, J. (ed.). 1983. 171-206.

Murdoch, B.O. & U.I. Murdoch 1978. "The role of women in the 'Ealing course in German'". In Freudenstein, R. (ed.). 1978. 85-91.

Nalibov, K.L. 1973. Genus versus sexus: Professional titles, working titles and surnames for women in contemporary Polish. Bern: Herbert Lang and Frankfurt/M.: Peter Lang.

Newmeyer, F.J. 1983. Grammatical theory: Its limits and possibilities. Chicago: The University of Chicago Press.

Nicholson, J. 1984. Men and women: How different are they? Oxford: Oxford University Press.

Nilsen, A.P. 1979. "You'll never be the man your mother was, and other truisms". ETC.: A Review of General Semantics 36. 365-370.

Nowacka, E. 1976. Temat na pracę doktorską. Warszawa: Czytelnik.

Orasanu, J., M.K. Slater & L.L. Adler (eds). 1979. Annals of the New York Academy of Sciences 327. Language, sex and gender: Does 'la difference' make a difference?

Pawłowski, T. 1983. "Rachunek sumienia dla zniechęconych". W drodze 5/1983. 77-84.

Pieper, U. 1984. "Is parental language sexually differentiated?". Studia Anglica Posnaniensia 17. 71-80.

Pisarkowa, K. 1979. "Jak się tytulujemy i zwracamy do drugich". Język Polski 59. 5-17.

Przylubscy, E. & F. 1983. Język polski na co dzień. Warszawa: Wiedza Powszechna.

Radgowski, M. 1982. "Konflikt płci". Kobieta i Życie 30/1640. 14.

Radgowski, M. 1983. "Celnik nie jest królem życia". Kobieta i Życie 51/1700. 5.

Rees-Parnall, H. 1978. "Women in the world of 'Kernel lessons intermediate'". In Freudenstein, R. (ed.). 1978. 119-121.

Rem, J. 1984. Felietony dla cudzych żon. Warszawa: Czytelnik.

Rickel, A.U. & L.M. Grant 1979. "Sex role stereotypes in the mass media and schools: Five consistent themes". International Journal of Women's Studies 2/2. 164-179.

Rieber, R.W., W. Wiedemann & J. D'Amato 1979. "Obscenity: Its frequency and context of usage as compared in males, nonfeminist females, and feminist females". Journal of Psycholinguistic Research 8/3. 201-223.

Riley, P. 1981. "Towards a contrastive pragmalinguistics". In Fisiak, J. (ed.). 1981. 121-146.

Rothstein, R.A. 1976. "Uwagi o rodzaju gramatycznym i cechach semantycznych wyrazów". Język Polski 56. 241-254.

Rowlands, K.E. 1979. Management English: Course book. London: Hodder and Stoughton.

Ryan, E.B. & H. Giles (eds). 1982. Attitudes towards language variation: Social and applied contexts. London: Edward Arnold.

Saporta, S. 1979. "Sexist language and the competence/performance distinction". In Brogyanyi, B. (ed.). 1979. 749-753.

Sartori Stein, A. 1978. "Cultural chauvinism in foreign language classroom". In Freudenstein, R. (ed.). 1978. 123-136.

Saville-Troike, M. 1982. The ethnography of communication: An introduction. Oxford: Basil Blackwell.

Schneider, J.W. & S.L. Hacker 1973. "Sex role imagery and use of the generic 'man' in introductory texts: A case in the sociology of sociology". American Sociologist 8. 12-18.

Scott, Foresman Company. 1972. "Guidelines for improving the image of women in textbooks". Glenview, Ill.

Scott, K.P. 1980. "Perceptions of communication competence: What's good for the goose is not good for the gander". Women's Studies International Quarterly 3. 199-208.

Sękalska, D. 1982. Kobieta wyzwolona? Warszawa: Krajowa Agencja Wydawnicza.

Schubert, K. 1985. "Ist Höflichkeit ungrammatisch?: Über formale und begriffliche Einheiten im Bereich der Personendeixis". In Kürschner, W. & R. Vogt (eds). 1985. 151-162.

Schulz, M. 1975. "The semantic derogation of women". In Thorne, B. & N. Henley (eds). 1975. 64-75.

Shores, D.L. & C.P. Hines (eds). 1977. Papers in language variation. Birmingham: University of Alabama Press.

Silveira, J. 1980. "Generic masculine words and thinking". Women's Studies International Quarterly 3. 165-178.

Skorupka, S., H. Auderska & Z. Łempicka (eds). 1968. Mały słownik języka polskiego. Warszawa: Państwowe Wydawnictwo Naukowe.

Skowron, S. (ed.). 1973. Podręcznik biologii. Warszawa: Państwowy Zakład Wydawnictw Lekarskich.

Smith, P.M. 1985. Language, the sexes and society. Oxford: Basil Blackwell.

Smólska, J. & A. Zawadzka 1969^2. We learn English II. Warszawa: Państwowy Zakład Wydawnictw Szkolnych.

Smólska, J. & A. Zawadzka 1970^5. We learn English I. Warszawa: Państwowy Zakład Wydawnictw Szkolnych.

Smólska, J. & A. Zawadzka $1973a^5$. We learn English III. Warszawa: Państwowy Zakład Wydawnictw Szkolnych.

Smólska, J. & A. Zawadzka $1973b^5$. We learn English IV. Warszawa: Państwowy Zakład Wydawnictw Szkolnych.

Spender, D. 1980. Man made language. London: Routledge & Kegan Paul.

Stanley, J.P. 1977. "Paradigmatic woman: The prostitute". In Shores, D.C. & C.P. Hines (eds). 1977.

Stanley, J.P. 1978. "Sexist grammar". College English 39 (7). 800-811.

Stern, R.H. 1976. "Review article: Sexism in foreign language textbooks". Foreign Language Annals 9/4. 294-299.

Stone, G. 1981. "Pronominal address in Polish". International Journal of Slavic Linguistics and Poetics 23. 55-76.

Stopa, R. 1983. "Czy tata to ręko-zbój - refleksje językoznawcy". Problemy 8. 41-42.

Strainchamps, E. 1971. "Our sexist language". In Gornick, V. & B.K. Morgan (eds). 1971. 240-250.

Sullivan, W.J. 1983. "Sex, gender, and sexism in English". In Casagrande, J. (ed.). 1983. 261-301.

Svennung, J. 1958. Anredeformen. Vergleichende Forschungen zur indirekten Anrede in der dritten Person und zum Nominativ für den Vokativ. Uppsala: Almquist & Wiksell.

Szkutnik, L.L. 1979a. English through problems 1. Warszawa: Wydawnictwa Szkolne i

Pedagogiczne.

Szkutnik, L.L. 1979b. English through problems 3. Warszawa: Wydawnictwa Szkolne i Pedagogiczne.

Szkutnik, L.L. 1980a. English through problems 2. Warszawa: Wydawnictwa Szkolne i Pedagogiczne.

Szkutnik, L.L. 1980b. English through problems 4. Warszawa: Wydawnictwa Szkolne i Pedagogiczne.

Szkutnik, L.L. & J. Pankhurst 1981a. The world through English 1. Warszawa: Państwowe Wydawnictwo Naukowe.

Szkutnik, L.L. & J. Pankhurst 1981b. The world through English 2. Warszawa: Państwowe Wydawnictwo Naukowe.

Szkutnik, L.L. & J. Pankhurst 1981c. The world through English 3. Warszawa: Państwowe Wydawnictwo Naukowe.

Szober, S. 1962^{12}. Gramatyka języka polskiego. (Edited by Witold Doroszewski). Warszawa: Państwowe Wydawnictwo Naukowe.

Tanner, N.M. 1981. On becoming human. Cambridge: Cambridge University Press.

Thorne, B. & N. Henley (eds). 1975. Language and sex: Difference and dominance. Rowley, Mass.: Newbury House.

Tokarski, R. 1978. "O kilku relacjach semantycznych w polu wyrazowym". Prace Językoznawcze 91. Z zagadnien słownictwa współczesnego języka polskiego. Wrocław: Zakład Narodowy im. Ossolińskich, Wydawnictwo Polskiej Akademii Nauk.

Tomiczek, E. 1983. System adresatywny współczesnego języka polskiego i niemieckiego. Socjolingwistyczne studium konfrontatywne. Wrocław: Wydawnictwo Uniwersytetu.

Townsend, R. 1976. Jak zdobyć szklaną gore organizacji, czyli co robić, aby nie tłamsić ludzi i nie hamować rozwoju. Translated by Stefan Bratkowski. Warszawa: Książka i Wiedza.

Trudgill, P. 1974. Sociolinguistics: An Introduction. Harmondsworth: Penguin.

Westfal, S. 1975. Teka językowa. Glasgow: Sikorski Institute.

Wisłocka, M. 1984. "Na pewno wyzwolenie kobiet ...?". Relaks i kolekcjoner polski 5/152. 5, 14.

Witczak, J. 1984. Kłopoty z miłością. 2nd revised edition. Warszawa: Instytut Wydawniczy Związków Zawodowych.

Wolfson, N. & E. Judd (eds). 1983. Sociolinguistics and language acquisition. Rowley, Mass.: Newbury House.

Wolfson, N. & J. Manes 1980. "Don't 'dear' me!". In McConnell-Ginet,S., R. Borker & N. Furman (eds). 1980. 79-92.

Zaręba, A. 1981. "Formy zwracania się do osób drugich w języku polskim i francuskim". Język Polski 61. 1-12.

Zimmerman, D.H. & C. West 1975. "Sex roles, interruptions and silences in conversation". In Thorne, B. & N. Henley (eds). 1975. 105-129.

Zwicky, A. 1974. "Hey, whatsyourname!". 1974. Chicago Linguistic Society 10. 787-801.

GRAZER BEITRÄGE ZUR ENGLISCHEN PHILOLOGIE

Band 1 Peter Bierbaumer: Der botanische Wortschatz des Altenglischen. 1. Teil: Das Læcebōc. 1975.

Band 2 Peter Bierbaumer: Der botanische Wortschatz des Altenglischen. 2. Teil: Lācnunga, Herbarium Apuleii, Peri Didaxeon. 1976.

Band 3 Peter Bierbaumer: Der botanische Wortschatz des Altenglischen. 3. Teil: Der botanische Wortschatz in altenglischen Glossen. 1979.

Band 4 Gerd Sieper: Fachsprachliche Korpusanalyse und Wortschatzauswahl. 1980.

Band 5 Rüdiger Pfeiffer-Rupp: Studien zu Subkategorisierung und semantischen Relationen. 1977.

Band 6 Bernhard Kettemann: Aspekte der natürlichen generativen Phonologie eines amerikanisch-englischen Dialektes. 1978.

BAMBERGER BEITRÄGE ZUR ENGLISCHEN SPRACHWISSENSCHAFT
(Reihe wird unter neuer Reihenbezeichnung ab Band 7 weitergeführt)

Band 7 Günter Radden: Ein Profil soziolinguistischer Variation in einer amerikanischen Kleinstadt. 1979.

Band 8 Karin Viereck: Englisches Wortgut, seine Häufigkeit und Integration in der österreichischen und bundesdeutschen Pressesprache. 1980.

Band 9 John Oakeshott-Taylor: Acoustic Variability and its Perception. The effects of context on selected acoustic parameters of English words and their perceptual consequences. 1980.

Band 10 Edgar W. Schneider: Morphologische und syntaktische Variablen im amerikanischen *Early Black English*. 1981.

Band 11 Val Jones-Sargent: Tyne Bytes. A Computerised Sociolinguistic Study of Tyneside. 1983.

Band 12 Lee Pederson: East Tennessee Folk Speech. A Synopsis. 1983.

Band 13 Cornelia Zelinsky-Wibbelt: Die semantische Belastung von submorphematischen Einheiten im Englischen. Eine empirisch-strukturelle Untersuchung. 1983.

Band 14 Rolf Bremann: Soziolinguistische Untersuchungen zum Englisch von Cornwall. 1984.

Band 15 Wolf-Dietrich Bald und Horst Weinstock (Hrsg.): Medieval Studies Conference Aachen 1983. Language and Literature. 1984.

Band 16 Clausdirk Pollner: Englisch in Livingston. Ausgewählte sprachliche Erscheinungen in einer schottischen New Town. 1985.

Band 17 Adam Jaworski: A linguistic picture of women's position in society. A Polish-English contrastive study. 1986.

Band 18 Mark Newbrook: Sociolinguistic reflexes of dialect interference in West Wirral. 1986.

Spiegel, Rotraut
DORIS LESSING: THE PROBLEM OF ALIENATION AND THE FORM OF THE NOVEL
Frankfurt/M., Berne, 1980. 173 pp.
Neue Studien zur Anglistik und Amerikanistik. Vol. 19
ISBN 3-8204-6021-7 pb. sFr. 33.–

The development of Doris Lessing's art from the traditional realism of her early novels to modernist works like «The Golden Notebook» and «Briefing for a Descent Into Hell» has been criticised as escapism. A detailed formal and thematic analysis of three representative novels shows that the modernism of Lessing's later work is a result of the author's radicalized understanding of our collective alienation. Far from indicating a betrayal of her humanistic commitment, it is a measure of the sincerity of this author's concern with the «ancient dream of free man».

Kessler, Heilgard
INDIVIDUUM UND GESELLSCHAFT IN DEN ROMANEN DER DORIS LESSING
Zum kontroversen Wandel eines Werkes
Frankfurt/M., Bern, 1982. 188 S.
Europäische Hochschulschriften: Reihe 14, Angelsächsische Sprache und Literatur. Bd. 106
ISBN 3-8204-6272-4 br. sFr. 44.–

Das Romanwerk der Doris Lessing ist bis 1969 von konstruktiven und kritisch-emanzipatorischen Elementen bestimmt. Diese Thematik zeigt sich besonders im Kampf des Individuums um Eigenverantwortung für sich und seine Welt (*The Golden Notebook*). Die späteren Romane jedoch entfernen sich, auch formal (Science Fiction), von dieser Thematik. Die vorliegende Studie stellt sich zur Aufgabe, diese Entwicklung kritisch auszuleuchten.
Aus dem Inhalt: U.a. Stufen des politischen Engagements – Die intrapsychische Reise – Der Konflikt zwischen Kunst und Realität – Lessings Science Fiction – Die Entpersönlichung des Protagonisten.

Verlag Peter Lang Bern · Frankfurt a.M. · New York
Auslieferung: Verlag Peter Lang AG, Jupiterstr. 15, CH 3000 Bern 15
Telefon (0041/31) 32 11 22, Telex verl ch 32 420